Building a Marketing Plan

Building a Marketing Plan

A Complete Guide

Ho Yin Wong
Kylie Radel
Roshnee Ramsaran-Fowdar

First published in 2011 by
Business Expert Press, LLC
222 East 46th Street, New York, NY 10017
www.businessexpertpress.com

ISBN-13: 978-1-60649-159-1 (paperback)

ISBN-13: 978-1-60649-160-7 (e-book)

DOI 10.4128/9781606491607

A publication in the Business Expert Press Marketing Strategy collection

Collection ISSN: 2150-9654 (print)
Collection ISSN: 2150-9662 (electronic)

Cover design by Jonathan Pennell
Interior design by Scribe Inc.

First edition: June 2011

10 9 8 7 6 5 4 3 2 1

Printed in Taiwan

Abstract

In any journey, if you don't know where you are going, how will you know when you get there? Equally, if you don't have a focus and direction for your organization, which is underpinned by realistic, actionable, measurable, marketing objectives and a good idea of how to achieve those objectives, then how can you grow your business and achieve long-term profitability? *Building a Marketing Plan: A Complete Guide* is a book that aims to provide a comprehensive, holistic, and practical framework for the essential business process of marketing planning. It is targeted toward students of marketing and business practitioners—marketers and non-marketers alike—and draws together elements of theoretical concepts, strategic thinking processes, latest research findings, and marketing applications in a straightforward, logical manner.

Demanding and savvy customers, along with a turbulent global business environment, require marketers to be highly sensitive to the environmental trends and capable of identifying the latest marketing opportunities and threats at an early stage. The successful use of processes and activities of marketing planning is crucial for organizations that aim to prosper over the long term. Through this text you will conduct an in-depth analysis of your current situation; develop a deep understanding of your target markets; set realistic, measurable, and timely marketing objectives; develop a series of marketing strategies based on four key elements of marketing; and ensure that you have considered efficient implementation and control mechanisms.

Keywords

Marketing planning, marketing plan, implementation, Boston Consulting Group, target marketing, segmentation, marketing research, positioning, consumer behavior, marketing objectives, SMART objectives, Four Ps, product life cycle, Ansoff matrix, marketing implementation, control processes, McKinsey Seven S framework, marketing strategy, branding, new product development process, pricing approaches, situational analysis, competitive analysis, competitive advantage, SWOT analysis, PEST analysis, marketing metrics

Contents

Illustrations

Figures

Tables

Foreword

Operating a business requires many skills. A business must have its goals and products; it must know its markets, operate efficiently, have good staff, manage those staff effectively and efficiently, adhere to many regulations and laws, and market effectively. Out of this mix, the business must produce a profit year after year. Since the mid-1900s the world of business has become more competitive every year—yes, every year. Never has this increase in competitiveness been more apparent than now, following the economic upheaval over the last 3 years. So, why do some businesses prosper while others struggle or fail? In many cases the answer is simple: Struggling businesses have no practical or effective marketing plan that optimizes and directs marketing efforts based on the actual marketplace—based on customers' needs and wants. It is this realm of marketing that is so often neglected.

Marketing planning is one of those areas of marketing that everyone knows we should do, but most businesses do not do. Of those businesses that do attempt to write a marketing plan, most fail to produce a meaningful document. One reason for this outcome is that few people know just what to put in and what to leave out. This monograph provides a complete guide with all of the essential elements—the must-have parts, but without all the unnecessary clutter that so many texts would have you believe is essential.

This text is aimed at two main audiences: the student taking a formal course and the busy business manager who needs to build a solid and practical marketing plan in an acceptable time frame. This is a difficult task. The authors have succeeded by bringing together in a single volume a practical approach and method, based on many years of experience. All of the essential elements of a marketing plan and the methods to follow are described using a nice balance of theory and practicality. This information is then embedded for the reader with a comprehensive marketing plan case study based on a real scenario.

The result is a text that provides the reader with a practical "can do" approach to market planning—a text that readers will find they continually return to year after year. I wholeheartedly recommend it!

Associate Professor Anthony Ward
Australia
January 31, 2011

Acknowledgments

We would like to sincerely thank the following people for reviewing the manuscript:

Kelly Choong
Lecturer, University of the Sunshine Coast, Australia

Professor Harish C. Chopra
Visiting Faculty, R. A. Podar Institute of Management, University of
    Rajasthan, Jaipur, India
Formerly Fellow at the University of Mauritius, Mauritius

Bob Green
Lecturer, CQUniversity, Australia

Assistant Professor Jia-Yi Hung
Department of Health Administration, Tzu Chi College of
    Technology, Taiwan

Ronda MacLeod
Lecturer, CQUniversity, Australia.

Professor Bill Merrilees
Department of Marketing, Griffith Business School, Griffith
    University, Australia

Barry Mitchell
Lecturer, CQUniversity, Australia

Associate Professor Anthony Ward
Adjunct Faculty, CQUniversity, Australia

CHAPTER 1

Introduction to Marketing Planning

We are involved in marketing every day as marketers and as consumers. When we get up in the morning, we encounter marketing. The alarm clock on the nightstand, the bed in which we sleep, the TV we turn on, the toothbrush and toothpaste we use to brush our teeth, and the list goes on. Marketing is defined as "an organizational function and a set of processes for creating, communicating, and delivering value to customers and for managing customer relationships in ways that benefit the organization and its stakeholders."[1]

In order to benefit the organization and its stakeholders, a customer-oriented approach needs to be established. A customer-oriented organization develops a win-win situation between itself and its customers by concentrating on satisfying customer needs and wants and achieving its own objectives at the same time. This is often called relationship marketing, as the organization monitors and responds to market information—including competitor actions and customer needs—with the view to building stronger relationships with its target audiences wherever possible. Market planning should be a means of building long-term relationships with customers through the development of a customer-focused mission statement and objectives and goals at the corporate through individual product line levels. It is necessary to examine all of these levels to implement the marketing concept and determine the appropriate marketing strategy to provide the right level of value to the customer.

This book is concerned with building a marketing plan that has the customer-oriented marketing definition in mind. In this book, we provide a framework for marketers to develop customer-oriented marketing strategies and plans that match an organization with its internal

Learning Objectives

After studying this chapter, you will be able to

- identify the stages in the strategic market planning process,
- discuss the benefits of marketing planning for an organization,
- identify the key components of the market plan and use these as a basis to start a plan,
- discuss market planning in a customer-oriented organization.

and external environments. In this chapter, we introduce the role of marketing planning by discussing the benefits and barriers of marketing planning, followed by the marketing planning process.

The Role of Marketing Planning

Marketing planning is the process that leads to an understanding of an organization's position in the market and a series of marketing decisions and actions to achieve an organization's goals within a specific time frame. The emphasis is on the process that includes tasks such as performing analysis, designing actionable strategies, implementing the strategies, controlling the whole marketing process, and setting up a time frame for the staff concerned. A marketing plan is the record of the activities from marketing actions, and it should be comprehensive, flexible, and logical.[2] A marketing plan can be considered a manual for marketing actions that is based on an analysis of the internal and external situations, clear marketing objectives and strategies for targeted customers, and management of marketing activities through implementation and control. It states where an organization is, where to go, how to get there, and by when.

The Benefits of Marketing Planning

Building a marketing plan can have a great, positive impact on an organization. There are five main benefits of marketing planning:

1. Marketing planning allows the marketers to thoroughly examine their internal and external situations with the aim of understanding the organization's overall position in the market.
2. Marketing planning forces the marketers to consider the needs and wants of their stakeholders, especially their target customers who provide sales revenue (for for-profit organizations) or other monetary and nonmonetary returns (for nonprofit organizations).
3. Marketers can utilize the planning process to systematically identify and evaluate a variety of scenarios, possibilities, and results.
4. Planning identifies the resources that will be needed to perform the planned marketing activities in order to achieve short-, medium-, and long-term corporate objectives.
5. Marketing planning helps marketers evaluate the results so as to revise objectives and marketing strategies if necessary.

In general, marketing planning can prepare marketers to have a firm understating of the business, its strategies, and the underlying factors that form those strategies. Given such a shared understanding, executives will be able to respond rapidly to new threats and opportunities.

The Barriers to Effective Marketing Planning

Building a marketing plan is not an easy task. In addition to the complexity of various marketing issues, marketers need to deal with potential barriers to effective marketing planning. There are a number of barriers[3] to marketing planning, including cognitive, procedural, resource, organizational, cultural, and data availability difficulties. The following is a summary of 10 of the main impediments to successful planning:[4]

1. *Confusion between tactics and strategy*. Managers might focus more on short-term tactics that help sell a product than on a strategy that aims at long-term sustainable competitive advantage. Managers often make the mistake that marketing planning is not required with short-term tactics. On the contrary, an organization with a strategic focus needs the assistance of the holistic approach of marketing planning to materialize the strategy.

2. *Isolating the marketing function from operations.* In order to overcome this barrier, marketers need to work with staff from other departments such as research and development and engineering to develop new products, accounting and finance to set appropriate budgets, production to deal with logistics and channel management issues, and sales departments to overcome barriers to effective selling and gathering relevant market intelligence. Top management plays an important role to ensure that marketers receive all necessary support and resources so they can perform marketing planning properly.

3. *Confusion between the marketing function and the marketing concept.* Some top management confuse piecemeal marketing functions with the holistic marketing concept. The former is concerned with separate marketing functions, such as advertising, customer service, sales, and product management, whereas the latter holds an inclusive view of marketing and integrates all marketing activities in a marketing plan that can satisfy the needs of selected customer segments in order to achieve the objectives.

4. *Organizational barriers.* Depending on the organization structure, an organization may be divided into various departments or units. Marketers face potential barriers when departments or units other than marketing or marketing-related areas are not interested in marketing planning. Other departments or units may have their own agendas to run their sections.

5. *Lack of in-depth analysis.* Organizations don't face the issue of too little information but rather a lack of information management. The major challenge is the capacity to provide in-depth analysis of the information available. Without in-depth analysis, marketers won't know where their organizations stand in the market, and the consequence is a failure to provide a strategic direction.

6. *Confusion between process and output.* Some organizations tend to make their marketing plans, the output, too bulky to be of any particular use. This is the outcome of focusing on the plan rather than the process. Some marketers mistakenly believe that a bigger output reflects a better process.

7. *Lack of knowledge and skills.* Some marketers rarely apply marketing concepts and techniques in their marketing planning. Some are unable to differentiate between corporate objectives, marketing

objectives, and advertising objectives. Adding to this confusion, communication and interpersonal skills often need to be strengthened or marketing plans will be ineffectively implemented.

8. *Lack of a systematic approach to marketing planning.* Within an organization, there may be different strategic business units conducting marketing planning. Consequently, each unit develops its own marketing plan. The variations of these plans might be caused by different levels of data analysis, different opinions on how to achieve corporate objectives, or perhaps different motivations of participating managers. The large discrepancy in marketing plans from different units makes corporate headquarters' coordination work very difficult, if not impossible.

9. *Failure to prioritize objectives.* Some organizations set too many objectives. There are too many subobjectives of subobjectives. One of the major contributions of marketing planning is to provide a strategic focus. Marketing planning should assist marketers to focus more on the important objectives and take out the trivial ones.

10. *Hostile corporate cultures.* Since corporate cultures are difficult to change and tend to maintain the existing power structure and the status quo, the introduction of marketing planning might create tensions that lead to changes in organizations. Resistance to change and office politics are often barriers to building an effective marketing plan.

Marketing planning is not a straightforward task, nor can it be completed in a linear, one-off manner. Marketers are likely to encounter various organizational, attitudinal, process, and cognitive barriers that hinder effective planning. Successful planning takes patience, knowledge, persuasion, and negotiation skills. Understanding the potential barriers to marketing planning helps marketers to be better prepared for the challenges ahead.

The Marketing Planning Process

The marketing planning process goes through four major steps, as shown in Figure 1.1. Step one is the situation analysis. The main purpose of this step is to understand where the organization stands. Step two is to analyze the target market so that marketers can understand the buying behavior of their target customers. This is followed by the step of setting marketing objectives and strategies. The final step is concerned with implementation of the strategies and evaluation of the results in terms of the objectives.

The cycle of a marketing plan is usually 1 year. Data gathering and analysis sometimes takes months to complete. Marketers need to factor in the time issue when preparing a marketing plan. In addition, as shown in Figure 1.1, marketing planning is a continuous effort rather than a once-a-year exercise. What follows is a brief summary of the four major steps. Each of these steps is discussed in more detail in later chapters.

Step 1: Situation Analysis

A situation analysis is an assessment of the environment in which the organization operates and of the organization itself. The former assessment is called external analysis and the latter internal analysis. The external analysis helps marketers identify the trends and changes of external factors, such as social, political, technological, economic, natural, and competitive environments, and develop an in-depth understanding of customers (current and potential). These external factors are beyond the control of the marketers. In the case of the external environment, the best marketers can do is understand the issues and adapt. On the other hand, the internal analysis is meant to assess internal factors that can be

Figure 1.1. Four steps to successful marketing planning.

controlled by the organization. The principal internal factors to consider are the organization's marketing, finance, human, and manufacturing resources, and the organization must develop knowledge of its management and organizational structure and culture. The situation analysis of the external and internal factors will lead to the construction of a SWOT (strengths, weaknesses, opportunities, and threats) analysis. The strengths, weaknesses, opportunities, and threats should be analyzed in relation to the organization's current situation and market needs. This analysis assists marketers to determine what the organization does well and what it does not. It also identifies the issues that need to be improved. We will discuss the situation analysis in chapter 2.

Step 2: Target Market Analysis

Once the marketer understands his or her organization's strengths, weaknesses, opportunities, and threats, the next step in marketing planning is to understand the markets and customers. Marketing information is critical in understating markets and customers. Two important tools are available to allow the marketer to gather marketing information. One is marketing research, and the other is marketing intelligence. Both tools generate marketing information for the marketer to understand consumer behavior—that is, who is buying or would buy what, and how, how often, where, when, and why that person buys. Marketing research goes through five steps: (a) defining the problem and the research objectives, (b) developing the research design for collecting information, (c) collecting the data, (d) analyzing and interpreting the data, and (e) reporting the research findings. While marketing research is usually conducted on an ad hoc basis, marketing intelligence is performed on a continuing basis.

Once marketing research has been completed, the organization must undertake the steps of the target marketing process: market segmentation, market targeting, and market positioning. Because resources are limited, the organization is unable to target every market. The organization has to divide the markets into segments that it can target. Segments can be classified on the basis of geographic, demographic, psychographic, and behavioral characteristics. Targeting is the evaluation of each market segment's attractiveness so that the marketers can focus on one or more segments that suit the organization best. Market positioning is a marketing strategy to place a product or brand to occupy a distinctive position in the minds of target customers relative to competitive products or brands. We will take a closer look at target market analysis in chapter 3.

Step 3: Marketing Objectives Setting and Marketing Strategy Formulation

After the target market analysis and segmentation, targeting, and positioning strategies are set, marketers can develop SMART (specific, measurable, achievable, realistic, and time-bound) marketing objectives and the various elements of the marketing mix can be deployed to provide value that will satisfy the needs and wants of the target customers. SMART marketing objectives state what products are to be sold to which markets—addressing market growth, market share, or profits. Marketing objectives should provide a tangible guide for action, provide specific actions to follow, suggest tools to measure and control effectiveness, be ambitious enough to be challenging, take account of the company's strengths and weaknesses, capitalize on opportunities and avoid or minimize potential threats, be well matched with corporate objectives and individual product line objectives, and have a specific time for completion.

The basic elements of marketing mix are product, price, place, and promotion and are sometimes referred to as the Four Ps (4Ps):

1. Product strategy is concerned with managing existing products over time, adding new products, and dropping failed ones. In addition, strategic decisions about the width and depth of a product line, packaging, and branding need to be made.
2. Pricing strategy tries to determine an optimal price for a product. Internal and external factors that affect pricing decisions should first be examined before deciding which pricing approach is to be adopted.
3. Place strategy, which is also called distribution strategy, focuses on the transfer of products from an organization to the target customers. The transfer may go through other organizations, such as wholesalers and retailers. The management of this transfer process

is referred to as channel management. Another strategic decision in relation to place strategy is logistics management, which is concerned with the physical movement of a product from one place to another.

4. Promotion strategy relates to coordinating an organization's communications and marketing messages between different media and ensuring there is consistency of the message throughout. The promotion mix elements (e.g., advertising, sales promotions, direct marketing, online and interactive marketing, among many others) all have different strengths and weaknesses that must be coordinated to provide an integrated message about the organization's products, brands, corporate identity, and social and environmental goals.

The four elements of the marketing mix are interrelated. The marketing mix strategies should be built on the basis of segmentation, targeting, and positioning with the organization's objectives in mind. We will cover the marketing mix strategies in chapters 5 to 8.

Step 4: Marketing Implementation and Control

The final step of the marketing planning process is implementation and control. Marketing implementation includes all the activities needed to make the marketing strategies work. Without a good implementation plan, marketing objectives are unlikely to be achieved, irrespective of how good the marketing strategies are. A McKinsey Seven S (7S) model is a practical tool to assist marketing implementation. The 7S model consists of structure, systems, shared values, skills, staff, style, and strategy. Marketers need to have a well-conceived and detailed 7S model in place to execute the marketing strategies.

The main purpose of control is to understand if the organization has achieved the predetermined objectives. The four major steps in a control process are setting standards of performance, identifying tools for measuring marketing progress, evaluating actual performance against the set objectives, and taking corrective actions if necessary. With the completion of the control process, a marketing planning cycle is basically complete and can be considered as the start of the next cycle. We will explore marketing implementation and control in more detail in chapter 10.

Marketing Planning in Action:
A Comprehensive Example

In order to show how to apply the marketing planning framework discussed in this book, a comprehensive example detailing all the marketing planning elements detailed from chapters 2 to 10 is shown in the appendix. The marketing plan example was developed for an imaginary company but is loosely based on a real organization for which we completed a consultancy project years ago. The example first introduces the background of the organization—Pindari Boomerang Factory. It then demonstrates the external environment analysis, customer analysis, internal analysis, SWOT analysis, and strategic decision analysis for the business. Marketing objectives, marketing strategies, and implementation and control systems are then developed in a step-by-step manner. It should be noted that the example intends to only demonstrate how to use the concepts discussed in this text to build a marketing plan. It is not intended to argue that the decisions and recommended actions are the only or the most appropriate ways to build a marketing plan.

As an introduction to the marketing planning process (and the layout for the remainder of this book), structure overview provides an overview of the structure and important features of a comprehensive marketing plan.

Overview of the Structure and Features of a Marketing Plan

Executive Summary. Provide an overview of the entire plan, focusing on recommendations and implications for management, competitive advantage(s), required investment, and expected sales/profits.

Table of Contents

List of Figures and Tables

1 *Introduction.* Introduce the organization's background, mission statement, and corporate objectives.

2 Situation Analysis

   2.1 *External Situational Analysis.* Include the PEST (political, economic, social, and technological) and natural environment analyses, looking for trends and changes in the macro environments specifically to expose potential opportunities or threats. (See chapter 2.)

   2.2 *Internal Situational Analysis.* Examine internal strengths and weaknesses, looking for resource levels, skills availability, marketing capabilities, research and development capabilities, management strengths, production capabilities, financial resources, and research and development potential. (See chapter 2.)

   2.3 *Competitor Analysis.* Examine competitors (both direct and indirect), looking for potential opportunities or threats (consider using a table to compare your products, skills, ancillary services, financial and human resource positions, etc. with those of competitors). (See chapter 2.)

   2.4 *Customer Analysis.* Describe the target market(s) and develop market segmentation information in detail, incorporating demographic, psychographic, and geographic descriptions. Develop market targeting and positioning statements. (See chapters 3 and 4.)

3 *SWOT Analysis and Competitive Advantage(s).* Provide brief summarized statements of the findings from the situational analysis.
(See chapter 2.)

4 *Marketing Objectives.* Conduct a product life-cycle analysis; Boston Consulting Group (BCG) matrix analysis; Ansoff matrix
analysis (explained in chapter 5); state competitive advantage
objectives for market leader, market follower, or niche market
positions. Develop SMART objectives that link directly with the
corporate objectives and the corporate mission; take advantages of
internal strength and external opportunities; and avoid or minimize internal weaknesses and external threats. (See chapter 5.)

5 *Marketing Strategies.* Precisely state how you will achieve each
objective by linking a target market segment with a marketing
objective and a product incorporating the marketing mix elements (the Four Ps—4Ps). (See chapters 6 through 9.)

6 *Marketing Implementation.* Calculate break-even points, budgets,
and returns on investments; compute sales projections and cash
flows on monthly and annual bases; evaluate the McKinsey Seven
S (7S) elements as they apply to your organization; and develop
actions/activities around each to ensure that your marketing plan
is appropriately implemented. (See chapter 10.)

7 *Marketing Control.* Develop marketing metrics to ensure that
your plan remains on track to meet the marketing objectives, and
corrective actions can be taken if needed. (See chapter 10.)

Summary

Marketing planning is the process that leads to an understanding of an organization's position in the market and a series of marketing decisions and actions to achieve an organization's goals within a time frame. Marketing planning is beneficial to the organization. It can assist the marketers to understand their businesses, strategies, and other related factors. Consequently, the marketers are better equipped to deal with threats and opportunities. Marketing planning is a difficult task. Marketers need to handle 10 major barriers to marketing planning. After removing these barriers, the marketers are more likely to develop a good marketing plan. The whole marketing planning process comprises four major steps: (a) situation analysis, including internal and external analysis; (b) target market analysis that indentifies the buying behavior; (c) marketing objective setting and strategic formulation clearly stating where to go and how to get there; and (d) implementation and control, ensuring the marketing strategies are executed as planned and evaluating the actual results against the marketing objectives.

Chapter Review

1. Describe the 10 barriers to marketing planning and suggest solutions to each of these barriers.
2. The 4Ps are the 4 basic elements of the marketing mix. Identify the 4Ps and describe the main aims of marketing strategies that could be developed based on each of these elements.
3. As the marketing manager for a medium-sized business marketing children's clothing lines, outline a marketing plan structure and briefly describe what you consider would be the main questions to address under each heading.

CHAPTER 2

The Situation Analysis

The situation analysis, or environmental audit, examines what is happening currently in the various environments in which an organization operates. It consists of an external audit—an analysis of the market, competition, and environmental factors—to determine potential opportunities and threats to the organization. The situation analysis also consists of an internal marketing audit—a review of the business's marketing, financial, manufacturing, and human resource capabilities—to determine potential strengths or weaknesses. This chapter discusses what to include in the external and internal audits.

Learning Objectives

After reading this chapter, you should be able to

- identify the components of a situation analysis,
- describe the two main items to be covered in an external audit,
- elaborate on the factors to be taken into account in an industry analysis,
- identify and discuss the factors to be incorporated in a macroenvironmental scan,
- outline what is to be included in an internal audit,
- explain the Internet-based approach to environmental scanning,
- explain the SWOT analysis and illustrate the elements to be included in such an analysis.

Scanning the Environments

The situation analysis is also referred to as environmental scanning or the environmental audit.[1] Internal (controllable) and external (uncontrollable) factors impact the organization's operations and plans, and a situational analysis of these factors will provide vital information for marketing planning. Figure 2.1 summarizes the factors to be taken into consideration for a comprehensive analysis of the organization's current situation.

The External Audit

An external situation analysis includes an analysis of the industry environment and the macroenvironment.[2] The industry environment is the more specific environment affecting the organization's product market segments, while the macroenvironment consists of the broader environments that impact society as a whole.[3]

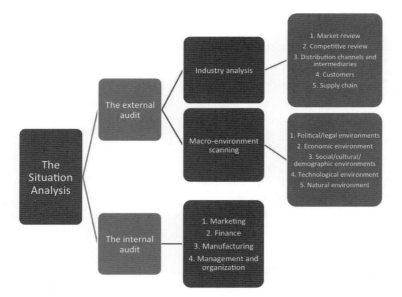

Figure 2.1. The situation analysis.

Industry Analysis

The following questions must be answered to conduct an industry analysis:[4]

1. What are the strategic aspects of the industry's structure?
2. Where is the industry heading, and what forces are driving it in that direction?
3. What does a firm need to know about the relevant economics of the industry in order to make money in the business?
4. What are the strategic problems and issues that face the industry?

The industry analysis needs to examine the following five interrelated factors:[5]

- Market review
- Competitive review
- Distribution channels and intermediaries
- Customers (end users)
- Supply

Market Review

Market factors are those that affect the demand for a product.[6] For example, population and income figures are market factors, since they determine the demand and, hence, the market for a product. At the very least, you should have an understanding of the market factors that influence the demand for your product, as future strategies, advertising programs, production schedules, capital expenditures, and human resource requirements are based on future demand.[7] A market review will include an analysis of the current situation of the market, historical trends, and future market trends. The market can be measured in terms of volume (units sold), value (value of units sold), and size of each segment within the total market.[8]

In order to estimate future demand, you should analyze historical sales data and perform a statistical analysis to better understand the industry trends.[9] Time series models may reveal seasonal, cyclical, or random variations in sales, as well as growth patterns. The estimation of demand may be affected by the following:

- Consumers' income levels
- Price and availability of competitors' goods
- Appearance of superior substitute products
- Advertising efforts
- Economic trends[10]

Several other techniques have been suggested to forecast market trends:[11]

1. The Delphi technique, in which a group of experts give and compare their opinions together about the future until a group consensus is formed
2. Marketing research tests, such as a survey of buyer intentions or new product market testing
3. Customer aggregation models, which break sales down into different components for which forecasts are made and then are multiplied together to get a sales prediction (for example, see Figure 2.2)

Figure 2.2. A model of customer aggregation.

4. Causal methods, such as regression analysis and input-output models, where demand is expressed as a function of a number of factors

Competitive Review

A competitor analysis is also a crucial element of the external audit.[12] The competitor analysis is designed to determine how the organization is performing in terms of its competitors.[13] In addition, the analysis forces marketers to consider differences and similarities in the organization's marketing. Such knowledge will provide an insight into developing potential defensive or offensive strengths.

The competitor analysis is essentially designed to achieve three objectives:[14]

1. It allows you to understand your position of comparative advantage and your competitors' positions of comparative advantage.
2. It allows you to understand your competitors' strategies—past, present, and future.
3. It factors greatly in effective strategy selection—the element that makes your strategies work in the real world.

In conducting a competitor analysis, both direct (e.g., similar products in the same market) and indirect (e.g., substitute products) competitors have to be considered, as well as current and potential competitors. Organizations can compete on a variety of attributes, including price, service, product differentiation, quality, and support services.[15]

When analyzing competition, three important questions need to be considered:[16]

1. *What are the current and past strategies of competitors?* Here, the competitors' mission, target markets, marketing mix, and budget are all reviewed. The effect of the competition on the organization's market share, growth rate, and profitability are also assessed.
2. *How is the competition performing?* The actual performance of the competition may be measured in terms of sales, market share, growth, profitability, return on investment, profit margins, and net profit.

3. *What are the competitors' strengths and weaknesses?* By understanding your competitors' strengths and weaknesses, you can identify opportunities and threats and potential areas to pursue a competitive advantage. Strengths and weaknesses should be assessed in terms of product and product quality, product innovation and technology, pricing, customer service policies, promotion, distribution channels, marketing capabilities, financial capabilities, and costs.[17]

The following are guidelines for conducting a competitor analysis:[18]

- Recognize key competitors in the market segments in which your organization competes.
- Analyze the performance record of each competitor.
- Study how satisfied each organization appears to be with its performance.
- Examine each competitor's marketing strategy.
- Analyze the current and future resources and competencies of each competitor.
- Predict future marketing strategies of each competitor.
- Assess the impact of the competitor's strategy on your organization.

Types of Competitive Markets

The four main types of competitive markets are shown in Figure 2.3, and these must also be taken into account in the industry analysis.

The type of competitive market in which you operate will impact on your promotion and pricing strategic decisions. Consumers' understanding and expectations of what constitutes a "fair price," for example, is based on what your competitors are charging. If you operate in an unregulated monopoly (e.g., Argyle Diamonds in Australia), then you can set prices at whatever you think your consumers will pay. If, however, you operate in an oligopoly environment, you will need to set prices commensurate with your competitors. We will discuss these ideas further in chapter 7.

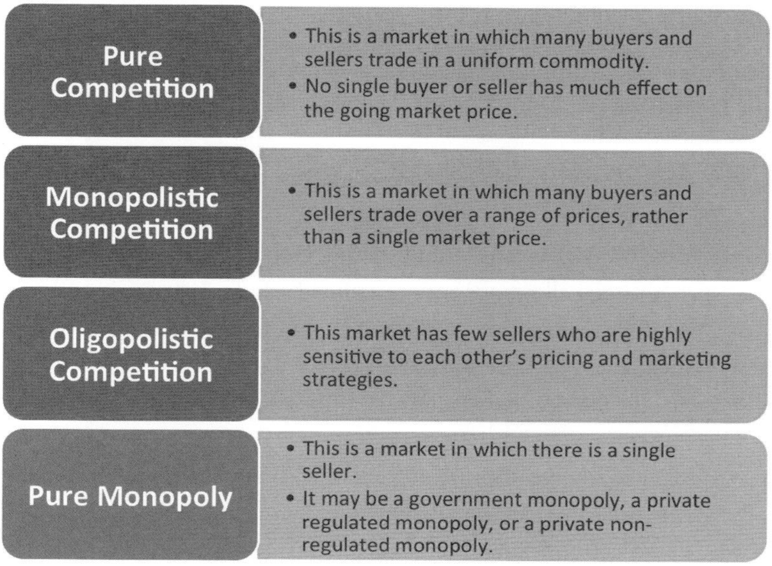

Pure Competition	• This is a market in which many buyers and sellers trade in a uniform commodity. • No single buyer or seller has much effect on the going market price.
Monopolistic Competition	• This is a market in which many buyers and sellers trade over a range of prices, rather than a single market price.
Oligopolistic Competition	• This market has few sellers who are highly sensitive to each other's pricing and marketing strategies.
Pure Monopoly	• This is a market in which there is a single seller. • It may be a government monopoly, a private regulated monopoly, or a private non-regulated monopoly.

Figure 2.3. Types of competitive markets.

COMPETITIVE ADVANTAGE

An effective competitor analysis will assist the firm in identifying possible competitive advantages the firm may have over competitors. A competitive advantage refers to those factors the organization excels in or has the potential to excel in over competitors.[19] A competitive advantage must be sustainable. Simply offering a lower price than competitors do is not often sustainable over the long term.

Competitive advantages are often in production, technology, natural resources, customer service, marketing, or management. Indeed, a competitive advantage can be almost anything that differentiates the organization's product from competitors' products. For example, Volvo has developed a very strong competitive advantage in the safety features of its vehicles. People do not think of a Volvo as a fast, sporty vehicle or a particularly fuel-efficient car (although these may also be features of the car). Instead, Volvo has focused its production techniques and marketing activities to position itself as the foremost vehicle manufacturer of family-oriented, safe cars. On the other hand, Ferrari has set out to position itself as a market leader in manufacturing sporty, fast, stylish cars. It is obviously not targeting the family-oriented or safety-oriented markets as Volvo does.

Distribution Channels and Intermediaries

The review of distribution channels and intermediaries should include information on

- distribution channels and intermediaries' operations and business practices;
- needs, wants, objectives, and trading conditions (margins, promotional allowances, product line fees, stock delivery, and inventory management requirements) of intermediaries;
- sales analysis per intermediary;
- strategic alliances between distribution channels and competitors;
- just-in-time inventory management and quick response automatic ordering mechanisms;
- use of electronic data interchange (EDI).[20]

Customers (End Users)

A review of customers or end users will include information on consumer attitudes and behavior and the various types of customers in the market. The analysis of customers will provide useful knowledge about the following questions:

- Who are the existing and potential buyers?
- Who is involved in the purchase decision process?
- What is bought?
- Where is it bought?
- Why and how do customers buy (the complexity and degree of involvement in the purchase)?
- How do customers view competitors' marketing mix (product, price, availability, and promotion) against the organization's marketing mix?
- What are the demographic, psychographic, geographic, and behavioral profiles of customers?

Supply

Industry supply can be defined as the ability of the industry to meet demand.[21] When determining future supply, the industry's capacity and how it utilizes that capacity must be considered. These will indicate the ability of the industry to satisfy demand. If long-term demand is forecasted to be significantly above maximum industry supply, you may want to invest in additional production facilities. The review of industry supply needs to include information on excess production capacity, the power of suppliers, and the likelihood of change (usually through breakthroughs in technology) occurring that will change supply conditions.

Macroenvironment Scanning

As shown in Figure 2.1 previously, five main macrolevel environmental forces impact marketing planning:

1. Political/legal environment
2. Economic environment
3. Social/cultural/demographic environment
4. Technological environment
5. Natural environment

It is essential that organizations monitor the changes in the PEST (political, economic, social, and technological) and natural environments and develop strategies to adapt to these changes.[22] A review can determine the opportunities and threats generated by each of these environmental forces in the future (for the next three to five years).[23] The review will first analyze, then diagnose each environmental factor—that is, first break it into a number of constituent parts to investigate their nature, functions, and relationships, then secondly assess the implications of the analyzed information in terms of opportunities and threats for marketing planning.[24]

Political/Legal Environments

The political environment should also be scanned for changes and possible impact of these changes on the organization. Factors influencing the political environment can include government policies; fluctuations in the value of the local currency of a country; military actions; recessions; nationalization, privatization, or deregulation; opening up of the economy; and so on.

The legal and regulatory environments must also be scanned to determine if any new laws or regulations have been, or will be, introduced that will affect demand or other marketing strategies. Usually laws are designed to protect organizations from each other and to protect consumers from unscrupulous businesses. Examples of changes that can occur in the legal environment are changes in legislation, taxation, duties or regulatory constraints (on product quality, packaging, labeling, advertising, pricing), and so on. These changes may affect businesses to a great extent—for example, the introduction of the goods and services tax in Australia resulted in catastrophic changes in the ways small, medium, and large organizations conducted tax reporting and paid taxes.

Economic Environments

In the economic environment, the organization must determine if any changes in economic conditions are likely and evaluate the possible impact of these changes on the organization or market. Changes in the economic environment can include changes in income, consumer spending patterns, inflation or unemployment, prices or materials availability, global business cycle trends, interest rates or foreign currency exchange rates, government policies for taxation rates, foreign investment, and so on.

Social/Cultural/Demographic Environments

The purpose of scanning the demographic/social/cultural environment is to determine the significance of population changes of the customers and their purchase behaviors.[25] These population changes can include the changing age structure of the population (e.g., an aging population), changing family structures (fewer marriages, more working mothers, fewer people in a household), changing education levels (a better-educated, white-collar population), increasing ethnic diversity in some regions or countries, and changing population levels in specific geographic regions.[26] Changes may also be occurring in consumer lifestyles, religions, and cultures.

Technological Environment

Perhaps one of the most obvious environments that impacts organizations is the technological environment, particularly in the electronics industries. The rate of change in technology has increased significantly in recent years and, consequently, the product life cycle of many products has been shortened. Technology affects aspects of products and production technology in particular and can change the way in which an entire industry may do business. We have seen the advent of the Internet, mobile phones, videoconferencing, and e-mails, as well as cost savings in production, and we have more to see in terms of robotics, biotechnology, communication technologies, transportation, computers, machinery, equipment, methods, systems, and so on.

The Natural Environment

Organizations should also consider the impact of changes in the natural environment and ecological factors. Extreme winters and summers can impact on various markets. For example, extreme summers are likely to have a positive impact on the sale of air conditioners and swimming pools, but they may have a disastrous impact on agricultural industries. Other markets such as the fashion and clothing industry and ice cream businesses are based on seasonal changes, and many tourism destinations only operate during particular seasons (e.g., ski resorts). The natural environment is also experiencing the following changes: (a) shortages of raw materials, such as coal, oil, minerals, and water; (b) increasing costs of energy with industrial development and economic growth; and (c) increased pollution. Governments often intervene in natural resource management in an effort to protect the environment. Emissions of carbon dioxide and other greenhouse gases are now being controlled following the Kyoto Protocol and the use of efficient cars, low-energy lightbulbs, and renewable and natural energy sources, such as solar and wind power. Also, using more efficient building materials is now being encouraged.[27]

The Internal Audit

The internal environment constitutes an analysis of the organization itself through its marketing goals and objectives, organizational resources, and internal structure and culture. The internal environmental analysis determines the organization's strengths and weaknesses in relation to the competitors' and includes an analysis of the current state of the marketing program, including its goals and objectives, looking for examples of the current sales figures for the organization. Questions to be answered in this section include the following:

1. Has the organization been meeting the proposed sales targets?
2. Has the organization reached the percentage of market share and profitability levels as defined by the overall corporate strategy?

The major areas for analysis within the internal audit include marketing, finance, manufacturing, management, and organizational structure and culture. The following lists areas for the internal audit.[28]

Internal analysis checklist:

1. Marketing
   - Marketing objectives and strategies.
   - Market share.
   - Sales (total, by geographical areas, by industries, by customers, by product, etc.).
   - Product quality, reliability, design, and technological superiority.
   - New product development.
   - Product life-cycle stage: Is the product/organization/industry in the introduction, growth, maturity, or decline stage of the product life cycle (PLC)? What are the current strategies adopted in this stage? Do they need to be improved? If the product is in the introduction stage and the organization is charging a high price for its product [a price skimming

strategy], should it change to a low price to attract customers instead and gain a higher market share? The product life-cycle concept will be explained in more detail in chapter 6.)

- Branding strategy (the position of the brand in the organization's portfolio), brand positioning (what the brand does or with what it competes), brand personality (the impression consumers have of the brand that converts the product from being a simple commodity into a unique idea that consumers identify with emotionally, rationally, or intellectually). This will also be covered in full details in chapter 6.
- Service quality.
- Pricing effectiveness.
- Distribution effectiveness.
- Promotion effectiveness.
- Innovation effectiveness.
- Geographical coverage.
- Marketing information system/research.
- Profitability analysis (current profits by products, markets, channels)/cost analysis of current costs or reducing costs
- Marketing procedures.
- Marketing planning system.
- Marketing control system.
- Marketing organization—formal structures (optimal structuring of marketing activities along product, market, and territory lines), functional efficiency (effective communication between marketing and sales; training, supervision, motivation, and evaluation of marketing staff), interface efficiency (how well the marketing department works with other internal departments). An organization needs to learn the symptoms of friction between the marketing department and other departments in the organization and take action to resolve these issues.[29] Other marketing department issues—including the lack of effective organization in the marketing department and the lack of knowledge, tools, and capabilities of the marketing staff to make the best use of technology—need to be monitored.

2. Finance
   - Cost and availability of capital.
   - Cash flow.
   - Financial stability.
3. Manufacturing
   - Facilities.
   - Economies of scale.
   - Capacity.
   - Able, dedicated workforce.
   - Ability to produce on time.
   - Technical manufacturing skills.
4. Management and organization
   - Visionary, capable leadership.
   - Dedicated employees.
   - Entrepreneurial orientation.
   - Flexible, responsive management and organizational structure and culture.

It is important to know the current state of the previously mentioned internal areas before the planning process can be started. This knowledge will help marketers determine the next stages where the organization wants to go in the future, given the current strategy. It will also help the organization decide on any new strategies it may need to maximize market share, revenue, and profitability.

An Internet-Based Approach to Environmental Scanning

An Internet-based approach to environmental scanning in marketing planning may outperform human experts in a typical scanning task.[30] Major breakthroughs or developments in technology, business science, politics, and society are published on the World Wide Web often long before their consequences can be observed in real life. A framework based on the information foraging theory (IFT) could assist in determining the relevance of documents and facilitating the automation of information search processes.

The SWOT Analysis

The strengths, weaknesses, opportunities, and threats (SWOT) analysis is the process of distilling the information that was collected during the situational analysis into a straightforward model to be used as the basis for developing a workable marketing plan. Some authors maintain that the SWOT analysis should be determined in relation to competitors' SWOT. For instance, strengths and weaknesses will include not only the strengths and weaknesses of the organization but also those of its competitors. Nevertheless, an assessment of SWOT is essential to complete the analysis of competitors.

Strengths and weaknesses tend to be internal and have to do with the past or the present. Opportunities and threats tend to be external to the organization and have to do with the future.

Internal Factors

Strengths. What the organization is good at, the strengths of its product and service, what it does best. Once the critical success factors where the organization has particular strengths are identified, the potential areas for establishing a sustainable competitive advantage can be determined.

Weaknesses. Poor products, services, portfolio gaps, image problems, inefficient salespeople, inadequate distributor network, few organizational resources, factory location, lack of flexibility, and so on. The organization should identify ways to redress these weaknesses.

External Factors

Opportunities. Market growth or change, new markets, products or services, different ways of marketing the organization's products or services, mergers, changes in currency exchange rates, and so on. The organization should consider how these opportunities may be exploited.

Threats. Economic forces and competition, changes in legislation, changes of habits, new technology, high interest rates, and so on. As far ahead as possible, firms should make contingency plans for these factors.[31]

Summary

This chapter presented the situation analysis, including an in-depth examination of the internal and external audit processes. The internal audit is a critical evaluation of the organization's current and anticipated internal environment with respect to its overall corporate strategy and marketing objectives and performance, allocation of resources (both financial and human), and structural characteristics.

The external audit has two elements, namely an industry analysis and a scan of the macroenvironment. An industry analysis examines the current state of the industry and determines future directions. The industry analysis also reviews the market, competition, distribution channels and intermediaries, customers, and industry supply. A macroenvironmental scan, on the other hand, reviews these environmental factors: the demographic/social/cultural environments, the political/legal environments, the technological environment, the economic environment, and last but not least the natural environment.

The final and most important stage of the situation analysis is the SWOT analysis where the situation analysis is summarized. Here, the critical success factors regarding the organization's capabilities will be appreciated and built upon, weaknesses will be worked out, opportunities will be identified and exploited, threats will be recognized, and contingency plans will be established.

Chapter Review

1. Conduct a situation analysis of an organization with which you are familiar.
2. Conduct a SWOT analysis of that organization.

CHAPTER 3

Analyzing the Target Market, Part 1

Marketing Research

The next step in the marketing plan is to understand, define, and analyze the target market. It is essential to know who your customers are and what, when, where, why, how, how much, and how often they buy. Your product may not meet the needs and wants of the mass market, but rather a particular segment (or several segments) of that market. You would waste resources trying to reach the mass market if this was the case. For example, you could waste money when advertising and communicating the intended message to the wrong people, or when distributing on an intensive basis. It is, therefore, better to do the following things:

- Find out more information on your customers through marketing research.
- Target these customers through the market segmentation, targeting, and positioning process.
- Understand customers' buying behavior.

This chapter will cover the marketing research process, which is a bulky process, and the next chapter of the book will cover the subsequent aspects of consumer buying behavior and the market segmentation, targeting, and positioning process.

Learning Objectives

After reading this chapter, you should be able to

- define a market,
- define marketing research,
- explain why marketing research is necessary,
- identify the types of marketing research information needed for the marketing plan,
- discuss the factors that affect the marketing research budget,
- identify the internal and external marketing research resources,
- explain the steps in the marketing research process,
- explain the tools available for the continuous information process,
- explain what marketing intelligence is, and distinguish between marketing intelligence and marketing research.

Definition of a Market

A market is the set of all actual and potential buyers of a product or service. Customers in a market must have "a need, have resources, and authority to engage in exchange and must be willing to offer these resources in exchange for what they want."[1]

Marketing Research

The marketing concept suggests that the central focus of the firm should be the customer's satisfaction. Marketers can control a number of factors—the marketing mix—in attempting to satisfy customer desires. The marketer's essential task is to combine these marketing mix variables (product, price, place, promotion, people, physical evidence, and process) into an effective and profitable program. Unfortunately, not all the elements that affect customer satisfaction are under the marketer's control. While he or she can control the marketing mix variables, macroenvironmental factors, such as the competitive, technological, economic, cultural, social, political, and legal environments, are mostly beyond control. Therefore, the marketing planner has an urgent need for information about the target market and the firm's environment.

Marketing research gives the firm a formal link to the environment in which it operates. Marketing research has been defined as the function that links the consumer, customer, and public to the marketer through information.[2] Marketing research refers to procedures and techniques involved in the design, data collection, recording, analysis, and presentation of information relevant to a particular market used in making marketing decisions.

Why Is Marketing Research Necessary?

Today's business environment is highly competitive, and markets and customer needs and wants are constantly changing. Therefore, information about customers, competitors, and the changing environment is essential. Marketing research is used to describe the market, monitor how the market changes, decide on potential actions to be taken, and evaluate the results of these actions.[3]

What Type of Marketing Research Information Is Needed for the Marketing Plan?

We need market and product information for the marketing plan as per Table 3.1.[4]

How Much Should You Spend on Marketing Research?

The marketing research budget will depend on the amount and quality of information the marketer feels is necessary to achieve the objectives of carrying out the research. Different internal and external sources of information are available, and the marketer has to decide to do a cost/benefit analysis of these sources of information. Costs of marketing research are normally easier to estimate than the value of marketing research, which can be in the form of extra profits achievable through the avoidance of marketing failures or identification of marketing opportunities. While perfect information is very costly, marketers should ensure that the cost

Table 3.1. Useful Information From Marketing Research

Market information	Product information
• What is the size of the market? • Who are our main customers? What do they buy? How much do they buy? At what price? In which outlets do they buy? Who buys? Where are our customers located? What is their demographic profile? Why do they buy? What are their attitudes and perceptions toward our product(s), our advertising, and our promotion? What is the buyer's readiness stage? Which benefits are sought? How loyal are customers to our brand and competitors' brands? • Who are our suppliers? • What are the main products sold? • Is it a new, mature, or saturated market? • What are the channels of distribution? • Which communication and sales promotion methods are used? • Are there taxes/duties/import restrictions? • Are there legal implications? What is the patent situation? What are the product standards? What about trademarks/copyright and protection of intellectual property? • Are there new areas of market/product development?	• Who are the potential customers? Where are they located? • Who are the market leaders? • Do current products meet customers' needs? • Do new products need to be developed? • How is the organization perceived in the market? • Who are the competitors? How big are they? Where are they? Do they serve the same market as you? Which products do they sell? At what price? What distribution channels do they use? Do they have new products?

of research does not exceed the value of information expected from the research. Sometimes, information may be readily available at no cost (e.g., in the organization's internal reports). The marketing research budget will also depend on the level of accuracy of information required by the marketer. The greater the accuracy of information required, the greater the costs involved will be. Finally, the budget may depend on how much the organization can afford to spend on marketing research.

Internal or External Marketing Research Resources

Organizations can either have their own internal departments for conducting marketing research or hire outside firms, such as PriceWaterhouseCoopers, ACNielsen, Taylor Nelson Sofres PLC, Baltimore

Research, IRI, Survey Sampling Inc., SDR Consulting, or others, to help design, gather, analyze, and interpret information. While information gathered from internal sources might be less expensive to obtain, external agencies may be more professional and quality oriented and have more experience, time, and resources to carry out marketing research. The cost of hiring the external agency might be very high, though.

How to Plan Your Marketing Research

The marketing research process has five systematic steps, shown in Figure 3.1.

Defining the Problem and Setting the Research Objectives

Marketers should first decide whether to conduct marketing research. Information might already be available, costs might outweigh the value of the marketing research, funds might not be available, or the timing might be wrong to conduct the marketing research (e.g., where products are in the decline stage of the product life cycle).

Figure 3.1. Steps in the marketing research process.

When an organization decides to conduct marketing research, the marketing problem needs to be identified and clearly defined by both the user and the provider of information. It is generally acknowledged that a problem well defined is a problem half-solved, and this will save a lot of time and money in the long run.

A marketing research problem can arise from either of two main sources:

1. A gap between what is supposed to happen and what did happen (also referred to as a *real problem*). For example, our objective was to sell 10,000 shampoos in March, but we managed to sell only 5,600. What happened to cause this drop in sales?
2. A gap between what did happen and what could have happened (also referred to as an *opportunity*). For example, we sold 100 cars in July, but could we have sold 200 cars if we had adopted the new hybrid technology in our cars?

Problem definition involves converting the marketer's statement of symptoms into a list of probable causes and the decision alternatives[5] and finally the information issues. Consider the following example:

- The symptom may be that product sales are below target objectives.
- The list of all possible causes may include the economic recession, low incomes, competitors launching a new product, or changes in customers' needs. The researcher and the marketer should then narrow down the possible causes to a set of probable causes—the most likely factors causing the symptom. Let's assume the researcher and the marketer finally determine that the probable cause of low sales was that competitors offered a new product to the market.
- Next, management has to decide what it will do to gain back its market share. Decisions require alternatives, and in this case, the marketer may decide to do more promotion, improve the product, and/or change the price. The marketer will then have to anticipate the consequences of each decision alternative. For instance, if the price of the product is lowered, by

how much will sales increase? Marketers make assumptions when assigning consequences to decision alternatives. The assumptions in this case may be that the lower price will attract customers away from the new competitor's product or that existing customers have strong brand loyalty. It should be remembered, though, that a lower price leaves a lower profit, which can affect the organization's bottom line.

- Finally, how sure are marketers about their assumptions? If they are completely certain that they have enough information to support their assumptions, then there is no need for research and the problem may be solved by choosing the correct decision alternative. However, if the marketer does not feel confident about the accuracy of the existing information, then he or she should seek more information through marketing research. For instance, in our earlier example, customers may need to be surveyed regarding their brand loyalty to the organization's product against the competitor's new product.

After defining the problem, marketers need to state research objectives to identify what information is needed to solve the problem, and these will help researchers decide exactly what they must do. Suppose that a bank is concerned about how satisfied its customers are with its services. The research objectives in this case could be translated as follows:

- To determine the average level of customer satisfaction with the bank's overall services
- To determine the average level of customer satisfaction with each aspect of the bank's services
- To determine the demographic profile (e.g., age, gender, income group) of the customers who are least satisfied with the bank's services
- To identify aspects of the bank's services that need improvement
- To determine customers' attitudes toward the bank compared to competitors

Research objectives can be of three types:

1. *Exploratory research.* Gathering preliminary information to help define the problem and suggest hypotheses. For example, what are the possible reasons for a decline in our sales?
2. *Descriptive research.* Describing marketing variables by answering who, what, when, where, and how questions. For example, what is the market potential for a product? What is the profile of our most likely customers? From where do customers buy our products most often?
3. *Causal research.* Testing hypotheses about cause-and-effect relationships. For example, will an increase in our advertising budget increase sales? Will a price change affect customers' perceptions of our product?

A decision should then be made about the style and duration of research activities. For instance, will quantitative research (such as research information on how many people hold similar views or display particular characteristics) be carried out or will qualitative research (such as research information on how people think and feel about issues or why they make some decisions and behave as they do) be conducted? Will the research be cross-sectional (carried out at one particular point in time, e.g., in June), or will it be continuous (conducted repeatedly over a period of time, e.g., in June every year), so that comparisons can be made and trends identified?

Developing the Research Design for Collecting Information

The research methodology is the plan that will guide the collection and analysis of data. It includes information on four important issues:

1. The types of data to be collected
2. The contact methods to be used
3. The sampling plan
4. The questionnaire design

Types of Data to Be Collected

Two types of data can be collected:

1. *Secondary data.* This information already exists somewhere, having been collected for some other purpose, but may be used for the problem at hand.
2. *Primary data.* This information is collected specifically for the current research problem.

Researchers should start collecting secondary data that might already be available and cheaper to obtain. If secondary data does not provide sufficient information, they can move on to collect primary data.

Secondary data are available from the following areas:

- *Internal sources.* For example, the organization's sales records, budgets, profit and loss statements, database of customers, and so on.
- *External sources.* For example, government sources, such as the Australian Bureau of Statistics[6]; syndicated sources, such as the Roy Morgan Research Centre[7] providing reports on TV markets; ACNielsen ScanTrack[8] selling information on household purchasing; Arbitron's[9] radio listenership data; and databases such as Proquest, EBSCO, Factiva, LexisNexis, and Dialog, among others.

Primary data collection is usually more expensive and takes more time to carry out than secondary data collection. Designing a plan for primary data collection involves a number of decisions regarding research approaches, contact methods, sampling plans, and research instruments.

There are three main approaches to collecting primary data:

1. *Observational research.* This technique involves watching relevant people, actions, or settings. For example, we can observe and count how many people visit specific displays within a museum to determine which are the most viewed exhibits.
2. *Experimental research.* This technique is used to assess causal relationships. Groups of subjects are selected and subjected to different

treatments under controlled conditions, and group responses are checked for cause-and-effect relationships (e.g., test marketing of new products to determine if changes in taste, color, packaging, or pricing effect consumer perceptions or buying behavior).

3. *Survey research*. This technique usually gathers descriptive and quantitative information on people's knowledge, attitudes, preferences, or buying behavior. Survey research can be unstructured to collect qualitative data and to probe beneath-the-surface reactions of responses and guide the interview according to the answers. Or structured surveys can be used where all respondents are asked a formal list of similar questions or given a questionnaire. Focus groups and in-depth interviews are approaches that are used to conduct unstructured interviews.

Contact Methods

Structured surveys can be administered through a variety of contact methods, each with its own advantages and drawbacks. Contact methods that can be used include mailed questionnaires, telephone interviews administered over the phone, Internet surveys, face-to-face interviews (e.g., door-to-door and mall intercept interviews), and self-completion surveys.

Sampling Plan

Most of the time, it is too time consuming and expensive to survey a whole population (e.g., surveying the whole population of Australia). Therefore, marketing researchers select representative units of the population, called a sample, to draw conclusions about the larger population. The sample should be large enough to provide accurate results. The sampling plan addresses the following questions:

- Who or what is to be surveyed (the sampling unit)?
- How many people or units will be surveyed (the sample size)?
- How are the respondents or units to be chosen (probability or nonprobability sampling methods)? Probability sampling is a type of sampling in which each member of the population

has an equal or known chance of being selected in the sample. Probability sampling methods include simple random sampling, stratified random sampling, systematic sampling, and cluster sampling. Nonprobability sampling is a type of sampling in which each element of the population does not have an equal chance of being selected because the choice of respondents is dependent on the researcher's judgment. Nonprobability sampling methods include convenience, judgment, quota, and snowball samples.

Questionnaire Design

When designing a questionnaire, be careful to ensure that it provides the information required by the marketing research study. Follow the subsequent recommendations when designing a questionnaire. Questions should be easy to understand, free of technical jargon and ambiguous words, inoffensive, brief, unbiased, and in a logical order; they should not be leading (i.e., they should not encourage the respondents to answer in a particular way). The questionnaire may contain open-ended questions and closed questions, such as multiple-choice questions. The use of measurement scales that enable respondents to express the strength of their attitudes and opinions, such as the Likert, semantic differential, Stapel, and importance rating scales, is encouraged. Examples of these measurement scales are provided in Table 3.2.

After designing the questionnaire, surveyors conduct a pilot test to improve the rigor of the questionnaire. Nowadays, software programs or Internet sites such as Qualtrics[10] or SurveyMonkey[11] help create and administer surveys.

Collecting Data

The data are now collected using the data sources and methods detailed earlier. Interviewers and supervisors are recruited, trained, and briefed for data collection and control. Administrative systems should be set up to facilitate the data collection process.

Table 3.2. Likert, Semantic Differential, Stapel, and Importance Rating Scale Examples

The _Likert scale_ is a statement with which people are asked to indicate the extent to which they agree or disagree.

	Strongly disagree				Strongly agree
	1	2	3	4	5
I like the service provided by XYZ Co.					

The _semantic differential scale_ is a scale with bipolar words at the opposite ends of a scale, and respondents are asked to indicate their positions between the two extremes.

	Modern			X		Old-fashioned
This restaurant is	Excellent				X	Not good
	Cheap	X				Expensive

The _Stapel scale_ is a scale with numbers to indicate the intensity of responses.

Excellent service	−3	−2	−1	0	+1	+2	+3

The _importance scale_ rates the importance of some attributes from "extremely important" to "not at all important."

	Not at all important				Extremely important
	1	2	3	4	5
Shopping in a convenient location is					

Analyzing and Interpreting Data

Once the data are collected, it needs to be input into computer files, such as SPSS (Statistical Package for the Social Sciences) or Excel, and cleaned for data entry errors and any inconsistent answers from respondents. The data will then be analyzed using statistical techniques, the findings interpreted, and the conclusions drawn. Many statistical techniques are available that are very useful for understanding consumers' perceptions. For example, factor analysis, discriminant analysis, conjoint measurement, or multidimensional scaling can be used to analyze customers' perceptions about the relative strengths and weaknesses of competitive positions of alternative products or brands.

Reporting the Research Findings

The researcher then communicates the research findings to the marketing decision maker in the form of a written report and may also present the research in a presentation to management.

The Continuous Information Process

Many organizations believe information needs not only should be in terms of projects but should also be a continuous flow of information for their marketers.[12] Internal database marketing can provide a rich store of information on key customers, their demographic profiles, products they usually buy, in what quantities, when they buy them and where, and so on. Customer relationship management (CRM), an IT-enabled method, allows the organization to integrate data across multiple customer contact points for the purpose of developing appropriate offers to different groups of customers.[13] Data mining software also can be used to enable marketers to search for relevant patterns and can be used for market segmentation; causal, econometric, or predictive modeling; and undirected searching for correlations.[14] Last but not least, the advent of the Internet is one of the main facilitators of information sharing and communication.

Marketing Intelligence

Marketing intelligence is a set of procedures and sources used by marketers to collect and analyze publicly available and everyday information about developments in the marketing environment and on competitors.[15] It is a continuing and interacting structure of people, equipment, and procedures to gather, sort, analyze, and distribute relevant, timely, and accurate information to improve marketing planning, implementation, and control.

Marketing intelligence is gathered from many sources, namely the organization's staff, customers, suppliers, and resellers. Information is also obtained about competitors and developments in the market from business publications, trade shows, new patents, press releases, advertisements, web pages, annual reports, online databases, professional marketing research firms that sell data for a fee on brand shares, retail prices, deals, direct mail activity, media information such as radio and television audience ratings, traffic on different websites, and demographic analysis and projections by state, city, or zip code. Marketing intelligence serves four main purposes:

1. To assess and track competitors
2. To provide early warnings about opportunities and threats
3. To support strategic planning and implementation
4. To support strategic decision making[16]

While marketing intelligence is a continuing process, marketing research is conducted on an ad hoc basis when required. Marketing intelligence can thus regularly give valuable information on the target market to help in marketing planning, but marketing research will provide the information in more depth and with much more insight and details. Nevertheless, a study[17] conducted in Asia emphasizes the value of marketing intelligence because of its ability to continuously supply the important bases for strategic management decisions and, hence, the long-term well-being of the organization in relation to competitors and the environment. While marketing research is restricted in its scope because of its ad hoc nature and gathering and processing of data within a limited framework, this book argues that marketing research will have to become more analytical and integrated to offer total solutions to management.

Summary

Analyzing the target market is a critical component of the marketing plan, since marketing is about satisfying customers. Marketing research helps to identify the needs of consumers, types of consumers, and consumer buying behavior in the target market. In this chapter, we have elaborated on the steps in the marketing research process and on the need for continuous information and marketing intelligence.

Chapter Review

Assume you are working for an organization that sells hybrid cars.

1. Identify a target market for your organization's product. How would you describe the profile of customers in that target market?
2. Estimate the size of your actual and potential market in five years' time.
3. Suppose you need information on the target market and on your customers' buying behavior. What type of data do you intend to use for this purpose?
4. Where and how do you propose to gather information?

CHAPTER 4

Analyzing the Target Market, Part 2

Consumer Behavior and the Target Marketing Process (Segmentation, Targeting, and Positioning)

Today, marketers are moving away from mass marketing—trying to sell a single marketing mix to all potential customers in their markets. This may be because organizations may not have enough resources to supply the whole market, customer needs and wants vary, customers are geographically scattered, or their competitors are too strong in the industry.[1] Marketers need to understand consumer buying behavior in order to satisfy their customers by providing appropriate goods and services. Organizations are increasingly moving toward target marketing. This involves identifying market segments, selecting one or more of them to enter, and developing different marketing mixes to meet their needs. This chapter continues analyzing the target market from the previous chapter and covers consumer buying behavior, market segmentation, targeting, and positioning.

Consumer Buying Behavior

Marketing planners need to understand who buys their products; what they buy; and where, how, and why people buy their company's products. This insight can help marketers find how best to influence customers' buying decisions and activities and can result in the development of a

Learning Objectives

After reading this chapter, you should be able to

- discuss the two main theories affecting consumer buying behavior,
- explain the factors influencing consumer buyer behavior,
- illustrate the concepts of high- and low-involvement purchases,
- distinguish between the different consumer buying roles,
- explain why marketers are moving away from mass marketing to target marketing,
- describe the steps in the target marketing process,
- outline the benefits of target marketing,
- explain the requirements for effective segmentation,
- explain the four segmentation methods,
- differentiate between the three targeting strategies,
- explain market positioning and list the bases used for product positioning,
- discuss the items to be included in the marketing plan for analyzing the target market.

more suitable marketing mix for the customers targeted, leading to buyer satisfaction.

There are the two main theories of buyer behavior:

1. The first theory views customers as rational beings who purchase products that maximize their satisfaction or utility for the least financial outlay or the fewest opportunities forgone.
2. The second theory explains buyer behavior by describing the customer as a psychosocial person who is influenced by work, family, culture, reference groups, perceptions, aspirations, and lifestyles.

These theories do not, however, fully explain consumer behavior. The best way to explain buyer behavior is to assume customers buy products to gain certain benefits.[2] For example, a BMW car can be bought for its functional characteristics, its design, and its reliability or for acquiring a greater status in society. The benefits consumers are seeking from products are related to the factors that influence consumer behavior.

Factors Influencing Consumer Buying Behavior

Consumer purchases can be explained by personal, psychological, and social factors (see Figure 4.1).

- *Personal factors.* A person's buying decisions are influenced by personal characteristics such as their age, life-cycle stage, occupation, education level, and income.
- *Psychological factors.* Different consumers have different motives (such as possession, economy, curiosity, dominance, and pleasure), perceptions, beliefs, and attitudes toward what and how they purchase.
- *Social factors.* Consumers are influenced by social factors. When they buy, their tastes tend to be influenced by social class and culture, and their behavior tends to be affected by family roles and reference groups, such as friends or colleagues.

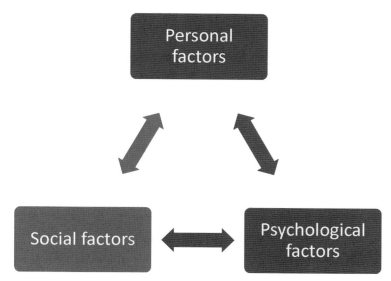

Figure 4.1. Factors influencing consumer buying behavior.

High- and Low-Involvement Purchases

When analyzing consumer behavior, it is also essential to identify the level of importance of the purchase to the consumer—the consumer's level of involvement with the purchase and the associated level of risk (financial, physical, and/or social) that is inherent in the purchase. The level of involvement will depend on the type of product and the amount of time available to buyers to make the decision on what to purchase. Consumers may make decisions that involve complex choices, or they may make simple choices based on learned responses. They may also make choices based on totally uninvolved and uninformed responses.[3] Usually, the more expensive, difficult to understand, risky, or important the product, the higher the level of buyer involvement and the more time and effort the consumer will spend looking for information and evaluating alternatives. Examples of high-involvement products are cars, houses, and computers.

Low-involvement purchases occur for products such as toothpaste, cereals, and chocolate. Low-involvement purchases require limited levels of information searching and have a low perceived risk associated with that purchase. Consumers use habitual decision-making processes—repurchasing products based on past experiences—and respond to environmental cues at the point of purchase. Impulse purchasing—making uninformed purchase decisions on the spur of the moment—is also a low-involvement process and is again influenced by point-of-purchase displays, in-store signage, packaging, and product placement.

High and low involvement result in different types of decision making, and marketers need to take this into consideration when planning. For instance, if the product to be sold is a laptop computer, which is a high-involvement purchase, customers will search for as much information as they can on the product, and marketers need to budget for providing all the technical information customers require in a format that is easily digestible, in locations where consumers can easily access the information—such as on the Internet, in the store, or from advertising, brochures, and so on.

Consumer Buying Roles: Who Buys?

Many buying decisions do not depend solely on an individual but are instead group decisions. For instance, when buying a house, a property agent may advise the family on the area where to buy the house, the wife may choose the type of house the family will live in, the children may like or dislike the houses they visit and influence the finalization of the contract, and the husband may be the one to make the final choice and make the purchase. People may play any of several roles in the buying decision (see Figure 4.2).

1. *Initiator.* The initiator is the person who first suggests the idea of buying the product.
2. *Influencer.* The influencer is the person whose advice or views carry weight in evaluating the alternatives.
3. *Decider.* The decider is the person who makes the final decision to buy.
4. *Buyer.* The buyer is the person who actually performs the purchase transaction.
5. *User.* The user is the person who consumes or uses the product or service.

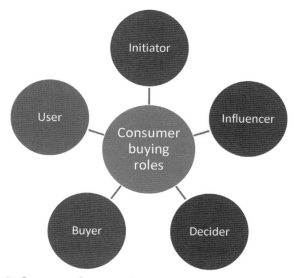

Figure 4.2. Consumer buying roles.

Consumer buying behavior—buyers' motivations, attitudes, perceptions, and the factors that influence their purchase decisions—provides marketers with a complex cocktail of issues to take into account when developing an appropriate marketing mix. However, understanding consumers is only the first step. Marketers must develop a tailored offering for individual consumer segments by completing the target marketing process.

The Target Marketing Process

By using an appropriate target marketing strategy, organizations can

- understand their customers' needs and buying behavior more precisely,
- allocate their resources more effectively with a minimum of waste,
- devise effective strategies and plans to meet the needs of the different market segments,
- assess their own strengths and weaknesses in relation to those of competitors,
- respond rapidly to changing market trends,
- identify gaps in the market where customers' needs are not being met.

The target marketing process consists of three steps, as shown in Figure 4.3.

As previously indicated, trying to provide a single marketing mix for a large, unsegmented market is often extremely expensive and somewhat "hit and miss." Organizations should begin to understand their consumers by dividing a total market (e.g., the population of Australia) into more manageable groups or segments.

Market Segmentation: Describing Consumer Segments

Four segmentation methods are commonly used in consumer markets, and these methods are useful in describing market segments in the planning process:

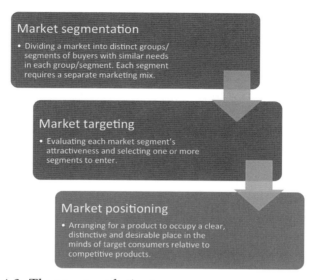

Figure 4.3. The target marketing process.

1. *Geographic segmentation.* In which country, state, region, city, or neighborhood is the customer located?
2. *Demographic segmentation.* What is the gender, age, income, race, or education level of customers?
3. *Psychographic segmentation.* What is the lifestyle (activities, interests, and opinions), personality, or socioeconomic status of the customers?
4. *Behavioral segmentation.* On what occasion do customers buy the product? What benefits do they seek from the product? For which purpose are they buying the product? For example, if the product is a cotton wipe, is it for baby care, medical use, or cosmetic use? Are the customers light, medium, or heavy users of the product? Are buyers in the segment ex-users, potential users, first-time users, or regular users of the product? Are customers "long loyals" (always buying the same brand, irrespective of price or competition), "rotators" (moving between two or three brands), "deal sensitive" (shifting between brands easily in response to price and promotion), or "price sensitive" (buying the cheapest product available)?[4] In which buyer-readiness stage[5] are customers: Are they informed and interested; do they want

the product; or do they intend to buy the product? What are the attitudes of people in the market segment toward the product: Are they positive, enthusiastic, indifferent, negative, or hostile toward it?

Requirements for Effective Market Segmentation

Segmenting a market is simply dividing a total market into specific segments. For market segments to be considered worthwhile, they should satisfy five criteria:[6]

1. *Substantiality*. A segment must be of sufficient size or profitable enough to make its pursuit worthwhile.
2. *Actionability*. The organization must have the necessary resources to design effective programs for attracting and serving the segments.
3. *Measurability*. Sufficient information should exist or be obtained cost effectively of the particular buyer characteristics. For example, the organization wants to sell a hair color product to the segment of redheaded people. However, no data are available on the number of redheaded people, and this segment is hard to identify and measure.
4. *Responsiveness*. Segments must respond differently to different marketing mix programs; otherwise, it is not worthwhile segmenting the market.
5. *Accessibility*. The organization must be able to reach the segment through its usual channels of distribution. Second, the organization must be able to communicate with its buyers in the segment. For example, it may be difficult to reach a segment of young men who do not read newspapers or magazines and watch less TV than other groups. The organization has to know which media are more appropriate to reach its type of market.

Market Targeting Strategies

After evaluating the different market segments and having found one or more segments worth entering, the organization must now decide which strategy it will adopt to cover the market. Typically, the three main market coverage strategies are an undifferentiated strategy, a differentiated strategy, or a concentrated or niche strategy.

An Undifferentiated Marketing Strategy

Here the organization pursues a mass marketing strategy by considering the whole market as a single market segment, and a single marketing mix is required that will serve the needs of the entire market. The organization's aim is to achieve economies of scale and cost with a single marketing mix. However, the risk is that not all customers will be satisfied. It is very rare to find the undifferentiated marketing strategy nowadays. For example, salt is a homogeneous product, but even in this case, salt producers have created market segments (e.g., selling table salt, iodized salt, cooking salt, and different brands of salt that engender loyalty).

A Differentiated Marketing Strategy

More often in today's markets, organizations usually decide to target different market segments, and this involves developing individual marketing mixes for each of the different segments. This strategy is used for products such as cars, detergents, and soap. For example, Nike sells athletic shoes based on behavioral and gender segmentation. Nike segments markets through different sports—such as aerobics, basketball, and football—by offering different products based on the age or gender of target markets and by segmenting through usage or occasion segments, such as walking, running, and cross-training. Such a strategy can result in more sales and greater customer satisfaction, and risks are spread across market segments. However, this strategy entails high costs associated with the different marketing mixes (e.g., in terms of R&D, production, marketing, promotion, distribution, and inventory).

A Concentrated or Niche Marketing Strategy

The organization might alternatively decide to serve only one or two segments of a market or niche. This strategy is commonly adopted by smaller organizations that are unable to compete in the wider mass market but can concentrate their limited resources on establishing a strong image and dominant market position within their chosen niche(s). Examples of niche marketing include shops selling petite or extra large clothes for specific size customers or budget airlines targeting the niche markets of no-frills travelers. With this strategy, the organizations keep costs down, as they have one marketing mix to manage and economies of scale are possible in production, distribution, and promotion. However, all the organization's eggs are in one basket, and if that segment fails, there is no fall-back position. The organization is also more vulnerable to competitive entry in the segment.

Market Positioning Strategies

Once marketers have decided which segment or segments of the market to enter, they must then decide what position or positions the brand or product should occupy within those segments. A product's position is the place the product or service occupies in consumers' minds relative to competitors' products or services. For example, Harrods is positioned as a high-quality department store in the United Kingdom, and in order to reinforce this positioning with its target market, Harrods makes sure that its product ranges, its displays, and its staff expertise are equally of high quality.

Organizations can use a variety of bases for positioning, and they must make sure to match their product characteristics to the target market's needs or wants. Bases used for positioning include the following:

- Product attributes (product features, customer benefits)
- Price and quality
- Product class (e.g., positioning a margarine brand with respect to butter)
- Use or application (e.g., using perfumes to attract women)
- Product user—a positioning base focused on the personality or type of user (e.g., Lucozade can be used by convalescent people and athletes)
- Against competitors (e.g., 7UP has positioned itself away from Pepsi or Coca-Cola so that the soft drink does not compete head-to-head with the market leaders)

After choosing a positioning strategy—for example, going after the "high quality with a high price" position—the organization must communicate and deliver the chosen position. For example, by producing high-quality merchandise, distributing through high-quality dealers, advertising in perceived high-quality media, and selling the product at a high price in comparison with competitors' prices, watchmakers Rolex and Omega are positioned as high-quality items against Guess, Jag, or Timex (see chapter 6 for further discussion on product positioning).

Summary

When analyzing the target market, besides conducting marketing research on it, the marketing plan should outline the buying behavior of targeted customers, how they make their purchase, what their decision making involves, what factors influence their buying behavior, what sources of information they seek, who makes and influences the purchase, and if it is a high- or a low-involvement purchase. Once a good understanding of consumer behaviors and motivations has been established, the target marketing process can commence. The marketing plan needs to describe geographic, demographic, psychographic, and behavioral profiles of the target customers. Market segments need to be substantial, actionable, measurable, responsive, and accessible. Following these guidelines will reduce the chance of segmentation failure. Market targeting and positioning strategies must then be established for the organization's product in the market.

Chapter Review

This activity follows from the activities in chapter 3, where it is assumed that you are working for an organization that sells hybrid cars and you have to identify a target market for your organization's product. Now consider and discuss these issues:

1. What targeting strategies would you adopt to reach the target market?
2. On which bases do you plan to position your product in the target market?
3. Which factors do you believe will influence the buying behavior of your target customers?
4. Which sources of information do you believe your customers will seek?
5. Who will make the purchase?

CHAPTER 5

Marketing Objectives and Strategy Formulation

Now that we have completed the situation analysis, we'll develop the marking plan itself. A marketing plan by definition means developing ways and means of achieving the corporate goals through utilization of the available resources and satisfying our target markets.

This chapter discusses setting marketing objectives in the market planning process. The objectives developed for the marketing plan need to be consistent with the business plan, the overall corporate strategic plans, or both. First, this chapter provides an overview of the nature of marketing objectives. Second, it discusses formulating marketing objectives, then introduces the different types of marketing objectives. Finally, the chapter covers the stating of marketing objectives.

The Nature of Marketing Objectives

Many authors agree that few steps are as critical in marketing planning as setting objectives. Objectives are designed to ensure the organization

Learning Objectives

After reading this chapter, you should be able to

- understand why it is crucial to set marketing objectives,
- develop and understand the Boston Consulting Group product-portfolio matrix,
- develop and understand the Ansoff product-market matrix,
- develop specific, measurable, achievable, realistic, and time-bound (SMART) marketing objectives.

knows what its strategies are expected to achieve and when a strategy has achieved its purpose.[1] Corporate objectives set the overall direction for the organization, while marketing objectives provide direction for the organization's marketing efforts. As the corporate objectives provide direction for the organization, these objectives need to be considered or adhered to when formulating the marketing objectives. The relationships between corporate objectives and strategies and departmental objectives and strategies are represented in Figure 5.1.

In simpler terms, corporate objectives are what the business wants to achieve, and they describe a destination or a result. Corporate objectives are often expressed in terms of profit. Profit satisfies shareholders and owners and is an accepted measure of efficiency. Corporate-level objectives, however, are essentially meaningless unless all departments work together to achieve these goals.

Marketing objectives are concerned with what products are to be sold to which markets. Marketing objectives may address desired growth, market share, or profits for products in specific markets. While there are no universally accepted standards or procedures for setting or measuring marketing objectives, as a guide, marketing objectives should[2]

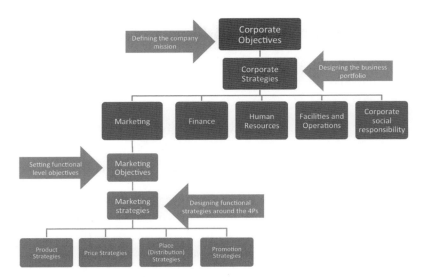

Figure 5.1. Relationships between corporate- and marketing-level objectives and strategies.

- provide a tangible guide for action;
- provide specific actions to follow;
- suggest tools to measure and control effectiveness;
- be ambitious enough to be challenging;
- take account of the company's strengths and weaknesses, capitalize on opportunities, and avoid or minimize potential threats;
- be well matched with corporate objectives and individual product line objectives.

Therefore, marketing objectives should provide specific, quantitative guides to what you will achieve and how it will be done. It is good practice to set short-term (up to one-year) and longer-term (two- to three-year) marketing objectives. Even if you do not have long-term planning, developing long-term objectives forces you to think about the future and consider the long-term implications of your short-term marketing objectives.

Formulating Marketing Objectives

When formulating marketing objectives, start with broad objectives and then concentrate on setting narrow and more specific strategies and tasks. Organizations may start with three sets of broad objectives:

1. Those that are easily attainable
2. Those that are most desirable
3. Those that are optimistic[3]

The easily attainable objectives will almost certainly be achieved; however, the organization should strive for those that are most desirable or even optimistic.

The Boston Consulting Group (BCG) Product Portfolio Matrix

A useful tool when developing marketing objectives is the Boston Consulting Group (BCG) product portfolio matrix. While profits do not always indicate product portfolio performance well—since they only reflect changes in the liquid assets of the organization, such as capital equipment, stocks, and receivables—cash flow is a more appropriate indicator of a organization's ability to develop its product portfolio.[4] The BCG matrix provides a graphic representation for diversified organizations to make decisions about their use of resources to support specific business units. The BCG matrix classifies an organization's business units according to its cash usage and its cash generation using market growth and relative market share.[5]

You can decide to plot business units, product lines, brands, or individual products. In our case, we will use the BCG matrix to examine brands or product lines, but the principles are the same for the other areas. Remember, though, the BCG matrix has limitations. It is not particularly relevant for public sector organizations, as market share and growth are not useful measures in these industries.[6] The BCG matrix may be drawn as shown in Figure 5.2.

An organization may have several products or product lines across a number of the matrix quadrants and would benefit from understanding the impact of their positions:

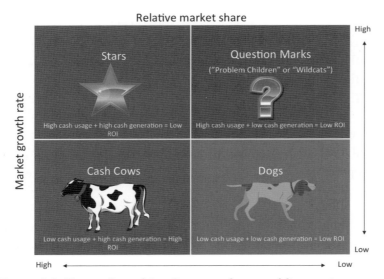

Figure 5.2. Boston Consulting Group product portfolio matrix.

- Brands or product lines classified as stars have great potential to generate cash; however, they are often expensive to maintain in this position. Stars often require a great deal of investment in promotion, research and development, and fixed and operating costs to maintain their market leadership.
- Cash cow brands or product lines have an established market and good cash generation. They are typically market leaders where there is little additional growth and do not require significant cash to maintain that position.
- Question marks have not yet achieved a dominant market position and may use a great deal of cash to push them into a star category, but they have high growth potential. Question marks are often referred to as "wildcats" or "problem children," as these brands or lines may be unpredictable in the market.
- Dogs often have little future. They have low relative market share with low growth potential. They represent a drain on cash reserves. If positioned closer to the cash cow quadrant, these brands or lines may be known as "cash dogs" and can usually be harvested—that is, they are allowed to generate as much profit as possible for no investment. If they are a "true dog," these brands or lines should be divested[7]—deleted from the product portfolio.

Relative Market Share Decisions

Different products and brands have to be managed differently. Like companies, products have strengths and weaknesses, and these strengths and weaknesses need to be balanced carefully to ensure that companies maintain market leadership, profitability, cash flow, and growth. The BCG matrix provides a powerful tool to visually assess the company's product portfolio position, which then provides indicators of the policies and objectives for each product or brand. An example of the BCG matrix as it may be used is provided in Figure 5.3.

In terms of market share, when plotted on the matrix, the relative size of the circle indicates the relative size of your company's sales volume in relation to your largest competitor's sales. You can also indicate the profit contribution of the product by including a segment in the circle.[8]

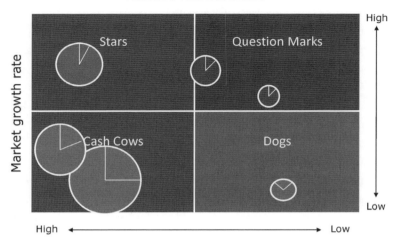

Figure 5.3. *BCG product portfolio matrix example.*

As you can see in Figure 5.3, the cash cow products' profit contributions are much higher than the star product.

Determining the relative market share—the position on the matrix for each product or brand—is a critical decision. For a simple calculation of the relative market share, divide your share by your largest competitor's share (volume of sales). A ratio greater than one indicates your product is the market leader.[9] Greater market share often (but not always) indicates a greater return on investment (ROI). For example, see Table 5.1.

Market Growth Decisions

Market growth decisions may reflect the stage of the product life cycle (PLC).[10] For example, star products are often in the growth stage of the

Table 5.1. *Calculation for Market Share Decisions*

Product	Your market share (volume of sales)	Largest competitor's market share (volume of sales)	Ratio
Product A	20	10	20 ÷ 10 = 2.00
Product B	40	60	40 ÷ 60 = 0.67

PLC, while cash cow products are usually in the maturity stage. Dogs are often in the decline stage, and question marks may be in the introductory or early growth stages (the stage of significant competitive turbulence). A further consideration here is the relative cash flow generated by each product or brand.[11] Stars have high cash generation but also have high cash usage. Question marks have low cash generation but high cash usage. Cash cows have high cash generation and low cash usage, and dogs generally have low cash generation and low cash usage.

To position your products or brands along the horizontal axis, you usually consider up to four criteria: (a) the size of the market, (b) the growth rate of the market, (c) the ease of entry into the market, and the (d) life-cycle position. Estimate which of these is the most to least important to your organization, awarding each a percentage value (out of 100%), and rate each of your products according to these criteria. For example, assume you have assigned weightings to each criterion as represented in the following table. For each product, the weightings don't change, but now assign a rating out of four against each criterion for each product. So for product A, the calculation of the market growth axis position would be as shown in Table 5.2. Using the calculations from market share and market growth, this product would then be plotted on the matrix as shown in Figure 5.4.

Table 5.2. Calculation for Market Growth Decisions

Criteria	Weightings (most important to least important)	Ratings for Product A (1–4 where 1 is unattractive and 4 is most attractive attribute)	Weight × Rating
Size of market	40%	4	0.40 × 4 = 1.60
Growth of market	30%	2	0.30 × 2 = 0.60
Ease of entry	10%	3	0.10 × 3 = 0.30
Life-cycle position	20%	2	0.20 × 2 = 0.40
Total	100%		2.90

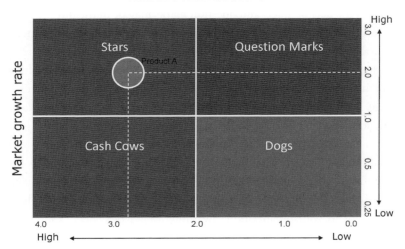

Figure 5.4. Product A location on the BCG matrix.

Objectives and Strategies for the BCG Matrix

Once you have established the relative position on the matrix for each product and provided circles that indicate your relative market share, the question remains as to what objectives should be set based on this analysis. The locations on the BCG matrix suggest a number of strategic options.

Stars: Invest for Growth

While star products may require more costs to maintain market leadership, products in this quadrant suggest that additional investment should be a priority.[12] Investment can be in the form of promotion activities, market research, further research and development on the product and its benefits, building production, and growing distribution networks. Marketing programs for star products should be aggressive with high-level selling, advertising, pricing, and sales promotion activities.[13]

Question Marks: Opportunistic Development

Products falling in the question mark quadrant should be targeted for selective investment.[14] Products in this quadrant show that your organization has strength in this category, but the market is not a high-growth area. Products in this quadrant can still provide good return on investment and may be able to be moved into the star quadrant with careful management. However, without investment, question marks have the potential to fall into the dog quadrant. Marketing strategies should include identification of niche or emerging market segments and targeted promotion activities to pursue.

Cash Cows: Manage for Earnings

Cash cow products also require careful management to retain their earning capacity, and selective investment can move them closer to a star product. This is an attractive market, as your organization has a high relative market share and therefore a great deal of business strength.[15] While the market may be in the maturity stage of the product life cycle, with further investment, you can gain further growth from this product. Marketing strategies should aim to maintain market share by promoting and expanding successful product lines and divesting unsuccessful lines or items. Promotion campaigns should be aimed at differentiation and maintaining or increasing brand awareness and loyalty in the market. Aim to maintain and keep prices stable with periodic sales and promotion activities.[16]

Dogs: Harvest or Divest

Cash dog products should be treated similarly to cash cows, where the low market growth opportunities are recognized and products are selectively harvested or sold to smaller businesses as niche market products.[17] Aim to identify and exploit niche growth market segments and improve production and distribution methods to gain cost savings. Products falling in the dog quadrant demonstrate that your organization doesn't have a great deal of business strength in this category; therefore, implementing significant investment of resources in this area is not wise.[18] With genuine dog products, divest by minimizing marketing expenditure and deleting items.

The Ansoff Product-Market Matrix

As a useful tool to help organizations further conceptualize their marketing objectives, the Ansoff product-market matrix essentially suggests that the competitive situation can be simplified to two elements: products and markets.[19] Therefore, marketing objectives are generally stated in terms of four possible actions:[20]

1. Selling existing products in existing markets (market penetration)
2. Developing new products for existing markets (product development)
3. Selling existing products into new markets (market development)
4. Developing or selling new products for new markets (diversification)

Figure 5.5 shows these four concepts. Each of the four possibilities is influenced by the growth of new technology and the increasing potential for new markets.

Therefore, marketing objectives are written with each of the four main actions in mind.

Market Penetration

With market penetration, the goals are to maintain market share, increase market share, or both. Market penetration is usually the objective for

Figure 5.5. The Ansoff product-market matrix.

cash cow and star products and is the least risky activity. Organizations can do this by increasing customer usage of products and selling greater volumes of products to current customers or by converting customers from competitors' products.[21] Common activities include developing customer loyalty programs and finding new uses for existing products. For example, with baking soda (a raising agent used in cooking) producers found that users also could benefit from the product by using it as a refrigerator deodorant, among many other uses. Companies released the usage information via websites and marketing campaigns and raised consumer awareness of the "new" uses for baking soda, thereby selling a great deal more volume of the product.

Market Development

Marketers can sell existing products in new markets by finding and developing new or emerging market segments or converting nonusers into users.[22] For example, bran-based breakfast cereals that have traditionally targeted mature-aged users are looking to convert other demographic segments such as children and teens to expand their sales in these new markets.

New Product Development

Developing new products to sell to current markets often means developing product line extensions (filling product line gaps or stretching the lines upward into higher profit segments or downward into lower profit or high-volume segments). New products can also be "new to the world" or modified products with new features and benefits or can be new to your business (such as in the case of your company buying new business entities). Marketing strategies include product launches into current markets with associated aggressive advertising, promotion, and pricing activities. New product development can be applicable for star, cash cow, or question mark products.

Diversification

Finally, diversification—developing or selling new products for new markets—is potentially the highest risk activity. Diversification became a catch phrase in the 1980s with unfortunate results for most businesses. Diversification was often interpreted as requiring businesses to bring completely new products (often by corporate takeover) into the organization. However, many organizations lacked competence in the new business areas, which often resulted in corporate failure and bankruptcy. The key to diversification is the relevance of the new products to your current lines. Can you use your current business strengths to support the new product? For example, if you have strength in distribution, then developing a product that can capitalize on the existing distribution networks is potentially a good opportunity. Equally, if you have a great deal of knowledge in baby boomer markets, can you further segment that market to better reach and service a niche or can you extend your market to accommodate Generation X segments with the new products?

Competitive or Differential Advantage

In chapter 2 we introduced the concept of competitive advantage in relation to the strengths, weaknesses, opportunities, and threats (SWOT) analysis, where for an organization to be successful, it must satisfy customer needs better than competitors do[23] and in a way that is sustainable over the long term. Based on the organization's size and position in the industry, it must decide how to position itself in relation to competitors to gain the best possible competitive advantage. Organizations can essentially develop two types of advantages in their industry:[24]

1. *Structural advantages.* These are advantages built into the organization such as low labor costs.
2. *Responsive advantages.* These are advantages that have accrued to an organization as a result of decisions over time, such as high levels of technological innovation or low production costs due to strategic upgrading of manufacturing equipment.

Essentially, organizations can adopt three main positions in their competitive advantage objectives: (a) market leader, (b) market follower or challenger, or (c) niche market.

Market Leader Competitive Objectives

Organizations that dominate a market such as Coca-Cola (soft drink), McDonald's (fast food), Google (Internet search engines), and Starbucks (coffee) can adopt one of several market leader objectives, usually in a bid for market expansion or market share protection.[25] These objectives are particularly for cash cow and star products and use market penetration and market extension strategies identified by the Ansoff matrix. More aggressive objectives can include preemptive strikes to attack competitors or discourage new participants from entering the market.[26] Major supermarket chains have been known to aggressively cut prices on fruit and vegetable lines, for example, to remove competition and prevent new entrants. Reactive strategies and counterattacks may also be used where the market leader aims to defend market share by reacting to competitor challenges or by challenging competitors head on or outmaneuvering competitors by moving into emerging markets before they can.

Market Follower or Challenger Competitive Objectives

Market followers or challengers are organizations that struggle with market leaders for market share.[27] For example, Pepsi Cola constantly challenges Coca-Cola for market share in the soft drink market, just as KFC and Burger King attack McDonald's market share in the fast-food market. Market challengers can choose aggressive objectives of head-to-head competition, counterattack objectives, and encirclement (moving against the market leader from several different directions by developing new products and encouraging customers to switch through offering new benefits and loyalty programs). Competitors also can develop less risky, reactive objectives of simply following the market leader.[28] Competitors offer matching products, prices, and marketing programs to generate a stable market share and reliable profits. For example, banks of similar sizes raise and lower interest rates and offer similar products and services to discourage switching.

Niche Market Competitive Objectives

The final competitive or differential advantage objective is that of niche marketing, which is usually adopted by smaller organizations.[29] Niche marketing objectives avoid directly confronting competitors by selecting smaller market segments and specializing in the markets they serve. Niche market segments may be based on geographic area, customer demographics (such as age or income), or price. For example, some insurance agencies only provide products for retirement age customers who are not working full time. Other car insurance providers target those consumers who only drive their vehicle occasionally by charging for insurance by mileage driven.

The SMART Approach to Setting Objectives

The overall aims of marketing are to maximize consumer satisfaction, maximize profit, and minimize costs (to the company as well as to the social and natural environments in which the company operates). In effect, marketing planning and marketing objectives should synergize the company strengths with external opportunities, minimize company weaknesses, and avoid or minimize external threats. Marketing objectives are quantitative commitments to performance for a specific period of time.[30] Therefore, an effective marketing objective must demonstrate the five key criteria shown in Figure 5.6.

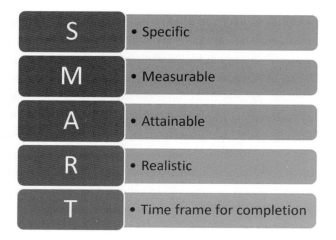

Figure 5.6. Setting SMART marketing objectives.

An effective marketing objective should follow the SMART acronym. It should be specific and measurable, it needs to be attainable and realistic for the organization to achieve, and it must include a specific time frame for its completion. The point is that marketing objectives (or indeed any objectives) need to provide enough information so that you and your organization will know what is to be achieved and by when. Then it is clear that if the objectives are not being met within the specified time frame, alternative actions can be taken to ensure success. If you don't know where you are going, then how can you possibly ever get there? A good objective should also assign a responsibility for the accomplishment to a specific area, department, or even an individual.

For example, a corporate level objective may be *to increase market share by 10% within 12 months*. A marketing objective aiming to achieve (or at least partially achieve) this corporate objective will be product and department specific: *The marketing department is to increase sales of product A to target market M by 10% within 12 months*.

This objective has the SMART elements and, as indicated by the Ansoff matrix, it deals with products and markets. It designates a specific product and a specific measure of success (sales), a goal to reach (an increase of 10%), a specific target audience, a time frame for completion, and a specific department for responsibility.

Types of Objectives: Some Examples

The previous objective is written in terms of sales but could equally be written in terms of increased revenue, increased value per sale, as a percentage of budget or profit, increased conversion rates, or any of a range of other possibilities. Also, marketing objectives need not focus only on sales or revenue generation. Considering the stages of the buyer-readiness model (introduced in chapter 2), we can write objectives based on product trial, awareness, or repeat purchase patterns. There are also differences in objectives set for retail, packaged goods, and business-to-business organizations.[31] These differences reflect the vast differences in the nature of these organizations.

Retail Objectives

Marketing objectives for retailers are primarily concerned with consumer behavior in a retail environment. Therefore, objectives often concentrate on increasing building store traffic, increasing transactions or the number of items per transaction, increasing dollar sales per transaction, increasing the number of multiple purchases, and improving repeat purchases among current and new customers. The following are some examples of retail marketing objectives:[32]

- Maintain market share leadership by increasing purchases per transaction of women 18 to 40, from 1.32 pairs of shoes to 1.57 pairs of shoes during the post-Christmas and back-to-school sales months of January and February.
- Increase value of sales per transaction among the current users by 5%, from $12.00 to $12.60 over the next 12 months.
- Maintain the current purchase ratio of 35% of first-time, online customers over the following 12 months.
- Increase traffic of primary market men 18 to 25 by 15%, from existing levels of 180 men per day, over the next 12 months. Maintain the current purchase ratio of 45% over the same period.
- Generate a two-to-one purchase-to-walk ratio among "tween" customers (children ages 8 to 12) over the next 12 months.

Packaged Goods Objectives

Packaged goods marketing objectives should also focus on consumer behaviors, but the emphasis is on two target markets: consumer markets and trade markets.[33] Marketers develop objectives to achieve sales targets by affecting the purchase rates of both trade customers and consumers. The following are examples of objectives set by a packaged goods company for the trade market:

- Increase trial of the travel agent market by 10% over the previous year for agents in the western region of the country over the following 6 months.

- Maintain current purchase rates of existing trade customers over the next year.

The following are some examples of consumer marketing objectives for packaged goods:

- Increase repeat usage of product W from 20% to 25% among current users over the next 12 months.
- Increase new trial of product T in the primary market, females 50 to 75, by 5% over existing levels during the next year.
- Grow the niche market segment share by increasing trial of product X among the secondary target market of males 18 to 25 by 10% over current levels within 12 months.

Business-to-Business Objectives

Marketing objectives formulated for business-to-business organizations concentrate on affecting the behavior of other businesses.[34] Business-to-business organizations often have many target markets. If this is the case, then every target market should have specific marketing objectives, which when added together will meet sales objectives. An example of a business-to-business objective for a construction company may be to maintain current reorder rates of concrete mix to existing customers in the northern region over the next 12 months. An example of a manufacturing organization objective may be to develop 12 new accounts over the next 12 months with average sales of $7 million per account.

Writing effective, successful, SMART marketing objectives requires a logical, disciplined approach. Give careful attention to your analysis of the BCG matrix, the product life cycle, and the Ansoff matrix. Concise, measurable, specific objectives allow you and your organization to quickly and clearly see where resources should be appropriately allocated to provide the best return on investment. Ensure that you quantify your targets in numbers and show specific products and specific market segments.

Introducing Strategies for the Four Ps

Returning to Figure 5.1, from corporate objectives and strategies, we have moved to functional level marketing objectives that show **what** you will achieve in line with corporate objectives. The next step in the marketing planning process is to develop marketing strategies to indicate **how** you will achieve these objectives. Marketing strategies are the means by which your organization will achieve the marketing objectives and are generally concerned with the major elements of the marketing mix—the Four Ps (4Ps)—products, prices, places (distribution), and promotion. The following chapters focus on strategies for these elements. In summary, a number of possible strategic options for each of the Ps can be considered (many of which have been raised in the previous discussion):

- Products
  - Expand or contract the product line, fill gaps, or stretch upward or downward.
  - Conduct research and development to alter features and benefits, quality or performance.
  - Standardize the product design or implement branding options.
  - Consider positioning or repositioning the product.
- Prices
  - Alter the price or terms and conditions of sale.
  - Implement price skimming or price penetration policies.
  - Implement sales promotions, discounting, or price bundling.
- Place (distribution)
  - Develop new distribution or delivery networks.
  - Consider adding or deleting channel intermediaries.
  - Develop online distribution facilities or other services.
  - Consider vertical or horizontal integration.
- Promotion
  - Change or develop advertising and promotion campaigns.
  - Consider the promotion mix elements (advertising, sales promotion, direct marketing, Internet and interactive

marketing, word of mouth, point of purchase, personal selling, sponsorship, public relations, and publicity), and change or modify the mix and focus of communication campaigns.

Summary

Few authors dispute the critical importance of setting effective marketing objectives. Indeed, the primary reason for failure of a marketing plan is due to inadequate marketing objectives and setting objectives without thorough analysis.[35] Without clearly formulated objectives, all sections that follow in the marketing plan will be of little use to management. This chapter highlights the importance of carefully defining marketing objectives in the plan.

Marketing objectives must be congruent with corporate objectives and are often formulated by developing broad objectives and then narrow, more specific objectives. Marketing objectives vary for retailers, packaged goods companies, and business-to-business organizations; however, marketing objectives are typically concerned with the profitability, market share, or growth of products and markets.

Chapter Review

1. Develop a Boston Consulting Group matrix for your organization. What are the key criteria you will use to determine relative market share? Review how you would position your organization's products and brands.
2. How do you define cash cows, stars, questions marks, and dogs?
3. For each of these categories of products, provide two examples of what actions you may take for each type of product. Can you justify each of your responses?
4. Based on the Ansoff matrix, what are the four general marketing directions that can be implemented for your products and markets?

5. Select a local organization that you are familiar with and work through the issues as a discussion.

6. Assess the mission statement and vision statement for your company. Develop SMART marketing objectives for your company based on your situational analysis, SWOT, BCG matrix, stage of the product life cycle, and Ansoff matrix analyses.

CHAPTER 6

Planning for Products and Brands

Because of the dynamic nature of the markets, organizations need to plan and develop existing products and search for new products in order to survive. New products introduced or tested on the market have a failure rate as high as 95%.[1] Thus it is imperative that every area of the product be carefully analyzed and planned so that continuing marketing decisions can be formulated from facts relevant to the total product.

Based on the situation analysis, and information in relation to segmentation, positioning, and buying behavior gathered from market research, you are able to plan your marketing mix. Planning your product strategy is usually the first step in developing marketing mix strategies. In other words, a product plan is not a stand-alone plan. It needs to be integrated with other marketing mix tools. While planning a product strategy, you need to understand the characteristics of the product, the behavior of the product life cycle, and the features that can create a strong brand. All these aspects need to be thoroughly analyzed prior to writing a product plan.

Learning Objectives

After studying this chapter, you will be able to

- appreciate the concept of product life cycle,
- master the new product development process,
- understand the concept of positioning or repositioning,
- identify the key decisions involved in branding.

Product Life-Cycle Decisions and Strategies

Sales of an organization's products tend to follow a typical pattern of development over time, named the product life cycle, as shown in Figure 6.1. Taking into consideration repeat purchases, not just first-time sales, the product life cycle attempts to recognize distinct stages in the product's sales pattern. These distinct stages are product development, introduction, growth, maturity, and decline.

During *product development*, a new product goes through various stages such as product idea screening and prototype and market tests. A new product may be dropped if it costs too much to produce or the responses are not positive from the market tests. *Introduction* is the period during which a new product is entering a market. The sales of the new product rise slowly. However, since organizations provide heavy promotion to inform and educate target customers, and there is significant need to develop initial distribution networks, this usually means a loss situation.

Growth is the stage where customers accept the product, distribution is expanding, promotion is heavy, repeat purchases are obtained from customers after initial trial, and positive word-of-mouth publicity spreads. Both sales and profits grow rapidly due to more customers and

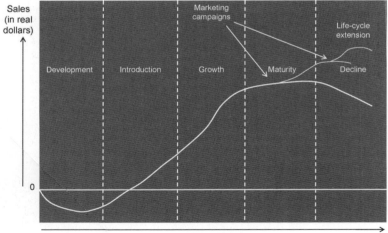

Figure 6.1. Product life cycle.

lower unit costs of the product. At the same time, market growth attracts competitors, most of whom either attempt to imitate or add new features to the already introduced product.

Maturity is the stage characterized by the extent of competition in the market. Product sales are stable or grow slowly, at best, since a certain amount of product loyalty is already established. There are three important attributes of mature markets:[2]

1. Repeat sales become much more extensive than first-time sales.
2. Customers are knowledgeable about the alternatives, so brand preferences become well established.
3. Few major technical advances will be forthcoming, so it is difficult to obtain technology improvement that can lead to a significant competitive advantage.

As a result, new organizations find it unattractive to enter the market while existing organizations struggle to increase their market shares. Price competition is a normal phenomenon at this stage since the market is already crowded with organizations.

Decline is the phase during which the product becomes obsolete and the loss of appeal to the customer results in sales decreases with the consequent rapid loss of profits. Two main reasons contribute to the decline of a product:

1. A better or a cheaper product enters the market that can fulfill the same need. The introduction of DVDs has pushed video cassettes virtually out of the market, for example.
2. Customers grow tired of a product—for instance, a shoe style.

Strategic Implications of the Product Life Cycle

The product life cycle can act as a planning tool, providing indicators to marketers about changes in behavior of a product, thus allowing marketers to react in time. In other words, the product life cycle can guide marketers who can adapt their marketing strategy to the developments of the product life cycle. It is difficult to generalize the most appropriate strategy for each stage of the product life cycle. Nevertheless, marketers might need to follow different strategies for dealing with the product in different stages of the product life cycle.

Introduction Stage

During the introduction stage, a basic product is introduced to the market. It is not a onetime effort. Marketers need to conduct continual research and development to reduce the product's imperfections. Further, efforts need to be made to enhance the product's value. A general formula to study the product's value from the customer point of view is

$$Value = benefits\ /\ required\ resources$$

Marketers can provide customers with better value by enhancing the benefits or by reducing the required resources, or doing both.

Growth Stage

During the growth stage, marketers need to compare their own product with their competitors' so as to improve the product. Marketers need to enhance the product's value with new features and benefits. Product lines can also be expanded to stimulate the growth stage. An example is the introduction of different flavors of chewing gum to expand an organization's chewing gum product life cycle. Extra services, such as a warranty, can be included in the product mix for manufacturing goods.

Maturity Stage

Common strategies available for marketers to deal with a product during the maturity stage of its life cycle include the following:

- Improving quality of the product with an aim to encourage repeat purchases and building customer loyalty
- Modifying the product to attract new customers
- Seeking new applications for the product (e.g., chewing gum may be marketed for use by smokers as a tooth-whitening product)

Decline Stage

Marketers face a challenging situation during the decline stage, but a number of strategies are available. Marketing and production programs must go through strict scrutiny to ensure efficiency. Marketers can rationalize the product line so that only the most competitive products are left in the range. If none of these strategies work, the last resort is to phase out the product. Pruning a product is not an easy task because marketers get attached to the product after a length of time, but bold actions are necessary to support a phaseout.

The Development of New Products

As discussed in the product life-cycle section, products often decline and finally may fade out. Organizations need new products to replace them to ensure growth. The product life cycles for many products are getting shorter on account of intense competition. Thus the task of developing new products becomes of even greater importance for marketers.

A number of critical issues must be examined for new product development. Marketers should continuously think about new products and cannot afford to wait until products reach the decline stage. Marketers also will need to ensure top management's commitment in terms of financial and organizational support to facilitate new product development. New product development is a continuous process, and competitors' products should be factored into the development process. An evaluation of competitors' products in the new product development process can have a far-reaching impact on achieving a competitive advantage. New product development should be futuristic and in line with changing market trends, and a product new to the organization may not necessarily be new to the market.

In principle, there are two main approaches to add new products to an existing range. One is to acquire products from other organizations, and the second is to develop new products internally. The first approach can obtain a new product faster than the second strategy. However, the organization might need to pay a premium to buy an existing product from another organization. Organizations have three main ways to acquire new products:[3]

1. By purchasing another organization or simply buying a product line
2. By obtaining a license or a franchise
3. By purchasing patents (however, this may be a cumbersome and lengthy process)

As previously indicated, developing new products in-house usually takes longer in comparison to the acquisition approach. However, the organization can learn a lot if develops its own new products. The new product development process can become knowledge capital for the organization that might give it a competitive advantage.

The New Product Development Process

Principally, new product development is a sequential process: "The new product development process involves a series of activities by which an organization generates new product ideas, evaluates them, and develops them into new products that enter the marketplace."[4] Facing three options at each stage, marketers must decide whether to proceed to the next stage ("go"), drop the product ("no go"), or seek additional information. The decision of "go" from one stage to another signifies further commitments of time and financial resources. The new product development process may be divided into six stages as shown in Figure 6.2.

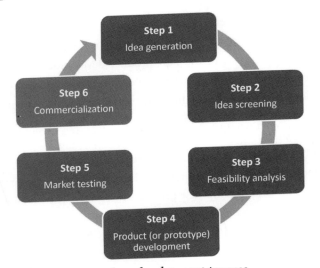

Figure 6.2. The new product development process.

Idea Generation

The aim of the idea generation stage is to create a pool of ideas for possible new products and to refine those ideas into precise concepts that are useful for specifying product design details and marketing plans. Idea generation is not a onetime exercise. It involves a continuous, systematic search for new product opportunities. Some organizations establish a new idea generation process that consists of a committee whose task is to meet regularly and develop all new product ideas. New ideas can come from various internal and external sources. The most obvious internal source is the research and development department. Other internal sources include the sales force[5], production personnel, and the customer services department. External sources are channel members[6] such as distributors and retailers, advertising agencies, universities and government agencies, suppliers, and competitors.

One of the most important external sources is customers. Customers should be the first in helping with new product ideas and can have significant input into the process. For example, customers might state they're unsatisfied with their experience of an existing product or describe how they modify a product to make it work better for their specific use.

Idea Screening

After ideas are generated, the second step in the new product development process is idea screening. The main purpose of screening is to determine which product ideas justify further examination. In general, a management team relying on its experience, tacit knowledge, and judgment screens the pool of new product ideas. A "no-go" error occurs when an organization discharges an otherwise good product idea because of a lack of vision about its potential. If an organization makes too many "no-go" errors, its standards are too conservative, the consequence being sacrificing potential profits. On the other hand, too many "go" errors will cost the organizations' human and monetary resources.

Feasibility Analysis

Product ideas surviving the screening stage are passed on to the third stage—the feasibility analysis. Some literature calls it the business analysis stage. The purpose of this stage is to estimate the profit contribution of the proposed new products in the long run. During the feasibility analysis, marketers need to identify new product features and estimate the new product's profit potential. The establishment of new product features allows marketers to avoid "me-too" products. New product ideas must possess product superiority in order to achieve sustainable competitive advantage in the market. To calculate the new product's profit potential, marketers need to first estimate demand in terms of sales. Sales estimation is based on the organization's assessment of the market size, competition, and the attractiveness of the new product's features. Then the cost of producing and marketing the new product needs to be estimated. Cost estimates include projections of manufacturing and marketing costs made by the new product development team. Based on the demand and cost estimates, marketers can determine an expected return on investment.

Product (or Prototype) Development

Once a new product idea has passed through the feasibility analysis, a prototype embodying the actual attributes of the product is developed. The major objective of this stage is to detect any potential production problems. Technical examinations are performed by the engineering and production departments to determine if it is practical to manufacture the product. This is an important step because what the new product development team can come up with and what an engineer can assemble in a laboratory are not necessarily the same things as what can be profitably manufactured. Moreover, lab tests need to be performed to decide whether the proposed product will reach or even exceed the minimum performance and safety standards. For example, Hasbro, a U.S. toy manufacturer, has a strict procedure to test all new products by a specialized team of engineers to ensure that they meet the safety and reliability specifications.[7] During this stage, the engineering and production departments attempt to refine the estimates of manufacturing costs and to acquire the budget for an expansion of production facilities if necessary.

Market Testing

After testing the new product in the laboratory, marketers need to test the new product in the market on a small scale, usually in specific geographical areas. The prospective customers, after trying out the product, are asked to provide feedback about their experiences and thoughts concerning the product. The duration of market testing varies from months to years. Market-test information, such as sales, buying behavior, and price sensitivity, is gathered and analyzed for modifying the product and the budget if necessary. Market testing can help marketers select the best marketing mix strategies for the official launch of the product, if there is a "go" decision after the market testing stage. There is a major drawback of market testing. Competitors can learn about the new products and are able to better prepare themselves for a potential competitive battle.

Commercialization

If a "go" decision is made after the market testing stage, marketers can plan to launch the product and commence the introduction stage of the product life cycle. The number of strategic issues at this stage include the timing to launch the product in the market, the number of markets to enter, and the width and depth of a product line to be offered. The product can be planned for a national launch, or it may be moved into the market in a step-by-step approach—that is, one geographic market area at a time. With regard to the timing of entering the market, marketers can choose from being the first to enter the market, entering the market at the same time as a competitor, or waiting until after a competitor has launched in the market. Being the first in the market brings benefits like "first-mover advantages," which provide the organization with the advantages of locking up with key distributors and customers, and gaining reputational leadership.[8] On the other hand, the advantages of allowing competitors to enter the market first are that the competitor bears the costs of educating the market, and the organization can understand the customers' acceptance of the product with the consequence of changing the product attributes, if necessary. The decisions in relation to these choices depend on the internal issues, such as resources and capabilities, and external issues, such as seasonality and competition.

Product Line Decisions: Width and Depth

Established organizations rarely rely on a single product. Instead, they market their products in terms of product lines. A product line is a broad group of products with common qualities such as physical or functional characteristics. When marketing many products, organizations face two strategic decisions: namely, product line width and depth. Product line width is the variety of sizes, colors, flavors, and models offered in a product line. Product line depth refers to the number of items of each type that are marketed. For a beverage organization, the product line width and depth can be depicted as in Table 6.1.

Product line decisions essentially involve choosing whether to add a new product item(s) to the product line or to drop a product item(s) from the product line. The former is called product line extension and the latter product line pruning. Product line extension can take three forms. An upward stretch is an introduction of new products into the higher end of the market (e.g., adding a premium beer in the beer product line). A downward stretch is an introduction of new products into the lower end of the market. A two-way stretch is the introduction of new products at both higher and lower ends. It is not an easy task to state the ideal of product width and product depth. Product line decisions are made on the basis of an organization's objectives, resource availability, and competitive advantage.

Product line pruning occurs when a product performs poorly. Before making a product line pruning decision, marketers need to consider the impact of the product to be pruned on the whole product line. The underperforming product may have strategic value in the product line. It

Table 6.1. Product Line Width and Depth of a Beverage Organization

	Product line width			
	Beer	**Red wine**	**Soft drinks**	**Energy drinks**
Product line depth	Light beer	Low alcoholic level	Cola flavor	General energy drinks
	Dark beer	Medium alcoholic level	Cream soda flavor	Sugar-free energy drinks
			Orange flavor	

completes the organization's product line. The presence of the underperforming product may send a signal to competitors that the organization will not surrender the market yet. The underperforming product may help to absorb part of the organization's fixed costs, irrespective of its below-average performance. Furthermore, some customers may still want the product. Leaving it in the product line may create goodwill and provide the organization with an opportunity to rejuvenate the product.

Positioning and Repositioning

Positioning is the image of a product or brand projected to the minds of the target customers in relation to competitors' products or brands.[9] It is a mind game. Two major issues exist in positioning. One is the projected image, and another is the competitive aspect. In order to effectively position a product in the marketplace, marketers need to have a thorough understanding of their target customers and competitors. Positioning is based on the concept of differentiation that can be in the form of physical or psychological attributes. A conceptual map is an effective way to show how positioning is conducted. It is a two-dimensional figure depicting how target customers perceive the various products offered in the market. Figure 6.3 depicts a positioning map for the watch industry.

On the positioning map, there are two attributes. Marketers can position their product based on the two attributes in relation to their competitors. Attributes should be chosen on the basis of what is considered to be important by the target customers and profitable for the organization. They can be based on

- services such as delivery, installation, rapid responses, and customer training;
- product differentiation such as product features, performance, reliability, and style;
- image differentiation such as symbols, events, and atmosphere;
- personnel differentiation such as courtesy, reliability, competence, and responsiveness;
- other attributes that target customers consider important.

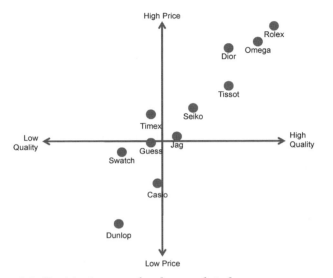

Figure 6.3. Positioning map for the watch industry.

Marketers can select a position that is far away from their competitors or one that competes head-to-head with a competitor, depending on the desirability of the attributes in consumers' perceptions. On the positioning map for the watch industry, Rolex, Omega, and Dior would all be competing head-to-head for the same type of consumer while Dunlop is positioned far away from competitors based on their location against the price axis.

When the performance of a product is not satisfactory or the product is at the maturity stage of the product life cycle, marketers can reposition the product with an aim to revitalize the product in customers' minds. Repositioning the product involves changing various marketing strategies, such as pricing, promotion, distribution, packaging, market segment, or even the sales team. By the same token, competitors can also reposition their products in order to occupy a sustainable position in the market. Considering the interactive nature of competition, positioning and conceptual mapping is not a onetime exercise. Continuous monitoring of competitors' activities and of the target customers' perception about the product is important.

Packaging

After a new product is developed, two product-related decisions should be made—they are about packaging and warranty. Packaging involves the design and production of the container or wrapper for a product. There are three major objectives of packaging: protection, promotion, and legal requirements. Packaging protects the contents in transit and while the product is in use. A package should be able to protect the product from leakage, compression, deterioration, evaporation, vibration, puncturing, and crumbling. A good package can prolong the product life on a shelf at the retail level. In addition to packaging for individual products, marketers need to consider the convenience in handling the packaging. Wholesalers sometimes might require extra inner carton boxes that can facilitate their delivery to various retailers. For example, instead of 24 items to be packed in an outer carton, a wholesaler planning to transport 12 items to two retailers may ask for two inner cartons (each with 12 items in it) to be packed in an outer carton.

Promotion is another major consideration for packaging decisions. Packaging can induce an impulse purchase and persuade customers to buy the product at the retail shops. It is especially important when the product is marketed in self-service stores. On average, a shopper spends 20 minutes in a store and views 20 products a second.[10] A package can be a silent promoter in a store. With an effective design, shape, and color, a package can catch the eyes of the shoppers in a second. The standard package has six faces that can be used to communicate with shoppers. These six faces can promote the product in the pack, present new uses for the product, provide further product information, or even cross market complementary products in the marketer's product line.

In certain situations, local laws may require marketers to disclose the product contents. An example is food. Nutrition information needs to be provided on the package (or label) of the product. The extent of information about the product's contents that needs to be provided to customers depends on the product type and the market. In addition to the product contents, some countries have legal requirements for bilingual or multilingual labeling on a package. For instance, all packages must show both English and French in Canada.

Branding Strategy

A brand is a name, term, design, symbol, or any other feature that identifies one seller's goods or services as distinct from those of other sellers. The legal term for brand is trademark. A brand may identify one item, a family of items, or all items of that seller. If used for the organization as a whole, the preferred term is a trade name.[11] Branding is a crucial part of product planning because, if properly deployed, it can provide marketers with a significant tool for differentiation to gain a competitive advantage. An unbranded product is just a commodity that is mainly sold based on price—for example, paper and chemicals.

Brand names are an integral part of branding. The brand name is the part of a brand that can be spoken in the forms of words, numbers, and letters. There are five main characteristics of a brand name.[12] A brand name should

1. suggest something about the product, particularly its benefits and use (e.g., Office Works and Exit Mould);
2. be easy to pronounce, spell, and remember (e.g., Mobile, Aim, and Surf);
3. be distinctive (e.g., 7UP and UPS);
4. be adaptable to additions to the product line (e.g., Kellogg, Ford, and Lipton);
5. be capable of registration and legal protection.

When legally registered with a government, a trademark (the brand name, brand mark, or trade character of an organization) offers protection for the exclusive use of that mark or name within the country where it is registered.[13] Together with the brand name and trademark, the design, symbol, and other features make up a brand. A brand can be developed based on physical and psychological attributes. Branding of products is believed to have three purposes:[14]

1. To conform to the legal patent protection the inventor may have
2. To guarantee quality and homogeneity in markets where buyers and producers cannot meet face to face

3. To differentiate products and services in a competitive environment

The first purpose indicates that marketers need to consider whether to legally protect their brands. Without legal protection, marketers risk infringement or even loss of a valuable asset. Registering the brand provides legal protection against competitors engaged in brand counterfeiting. Counterfeiting is "the unauthorized copying of the trademarks, labels, or packaging of goods on a commercial scale, in such a way that the get-up or lay-out of the cover, label or appearance of the goods closely resembles those of the original."[15] Even though legal protection of a brand is a barrier for other organizations to counterfeit the brand, high legal costs may be an issue for some organizations. In addition to legal costs, organizations need to set up a system to monitor the potential infringement of products. Coca-Cola staff visit retail outlets frequently to eliminate counterfeiting activities in the market.[16]

While legal protection of a brand may be useful, a better way is to provide target customers with emotional values. A brand can function as a quality assurance tool and can differentiate itself from competitors' brands to achieve a competitive advantage. From the customer's point of view, a brand can enhance purchase confidence and improve customer loyalty. Brands work by facilitating the customer's buying decision process. In a competitive market, customers face hundreds of products and messages competing for attention. Their buying decisions are reliant on their past experience and perception about a product, and this habitual buying process is associated with brand loyalty. Whether brand loyalty can be fostered depends on the brand value projected through the brand image in the target customers' minds.

Brand value denotes the branding efforts that build purchase confidence and create customer loyalty by adding distinctive benefits surrounding the tangible features of an organization's product or service. The concept of brand value is rooted in added value, which is claimed to be the most important part of a brand's definition and was used as the foundation for distinguishing a brand from a commodity.[17] The brand value goes beyond the concepts of tangible products. The psychological aspect of brand values distinguishes a brand from a product.

Essentially, brand value comprises three tiers:

1. Core functionality
2. Emotional values
3. Added value services[18]

The core functionality centers on the core physical product. Quantifiable measures, such as number of defects, usable product life, and use of the product in other situations, are forms of core functionality. Emotional values represent the intangible aspects of a brand that seek to fit the psychological profiles of the target customers—for instance, creating status and prestige for owners of the product or service. Added values are concerned with bringing in extra features and are critical to the brand, which would enhance the usage of the brand for the customers.[19] An example is the banking industry's reengineering of service delivery systems to reduce cost and time for the customer by using telecommunication technology. It is emotional values and added values that matter in creating branding value.[20] Brand value is critical in generating a positive brand image, which can help achieve brand loyalty.

Brand image is the "perceptions about a brand as reflected by brand associates that consumers hold in their memories."[21] There are two sources of brand image. One is a customer's experience with the brand, and the second is the information related to the brand. Customers gather information from what they hear, read, and learn about a brand. The information comes from advertising, word of mouth, publicity, sales personnel, packaging, promotion, and customer services. Customers also form perceptions of a brand image after consuming the product. These sources combined will give a brand an image that can be positive, negative, or neutral. Some images that customers associate with brands are power, sophistication, boredom, coolness, and class.

Brand Strategy Decisions

In developing a brand strategy, three approaches are available:

1. Family umbrella branding
2. Combination branding
3. Individual branding

Family branding is the use of the organization name as a brand for several or all product lines. Examples are Heinz, Campbell's, and Philips. This approach offers several advantages. The costs of introducing new products are much less, comparatively speaking. The marketing cost of creating brand awareness can be saved. Moreover, the cost of searching for a new brand name can be eliminated by applying the family brand to the product. A brand with positive brand image can facilitate adoption of the new product. In other words, a new product with a family brand can leverage the family brand to gain acceptance by customers and permeate the market faster. The major disadvantage of the family branding approach is felt in the event of a new product failure. An organization's overall brand image may be negatively affected. Thus organizations adopting the family umbrella branding approach endeavor to maintain a consistent quality among all products.

A similar branding approach to family umbrella branding is combination branding, which is the combination of individual brands with the organization name. Examples are Kellogg's Coco Pops, Kellogg's Crunchy Nut, and Kellogg's Special K. This branding approach enjoys the advantages of overall family brand image, but it suffers from the disadvantages of the family branding approach in principle if the organization carries any weak brands.

Individual branding is the application of different brands to different products in a product line. The Mars organization markets different chocolate products under different brands, such as Mars, Twix, Milky Way, Bounty, and Snickers. Similarly, Unilever markets personal care products under Dove, Pears, and Lux brands. A major advantage of individual branding is that one brand's failure will not affect other brands of the organization. Another advantage is that brands can be tailor-made to suit the characteristics of different markets. A new brand name, a different brand image, and a different variety of values can be adapted for each target market. A disadvantage of this approach is the need for heavy promotion for each brand. There is no spillover effect or economies of scale for the brands in a product line. This approach is best suited when products differ greatly in price, quality, use, and intended market segments.[22]

Summary

A product generally goes through five stages of its product life cycle. They are product development, introduction, growth, maturity, and decline. The stage at which the product is has significant impact on product strategy. In order to survive and compete in the marketplace, marketers need to introduce new products. The new product development process consists of six steps: idea generation, idea screening, feasibility analysis, product (or prototype) development, market testing, and commercialization.

A number of critical marketing management issues relate to the deployment of product strategy. Of critical importance is the development of the product width and depth. Product width refers to the variety of sizes, colors, flavors, and models offered in a product line, and product line depth represents the number of items of each type that are marketed. Positioning can help marketers to differentiate their products from their competitors' by projecting a distinctive image in the target customers' minds. Product strategy also involves issues such as packaging and branding. While packaging can provide protection to the product contents and promote the product, branding can assist organizations in achieving a competitive advantage by providing the target customers with brand values.

Chapter Review

1. Discuss an example of a real product that has gone through different stages of the product life cycle—for example video cassettes.
2. Come up with a new health-related product using the new product development process.
3. Develop a product line of liquid detergent for a market of your choice and justify your answers.
4. Design a brand for an all-wheel-drive vehicle covering all the branding issues mentioned in this chapter.

CHAPTER 7

Planning for Pricing

Price planning is the most overlooked area of marketing.[1] Rather, the organization places more emphasis on product development, advertising strategy, and distribution channel formation. Pricing decisions are thus quickly made without taking all the necessary market and cost factors into consideration. Pricing should be at the core of every business plan, since it is a powerful tool to increase revenue.

Price can be defined as a measure of the value exchanged by the buyer for the value offered by the seller. We would, therefore, normally expect price to reflect the costs to the seller of producing the product and the benefit to the buyer of consuming it. However, pricing decisions can be more complex, given that it requires knowledge of the market, competitors, economic conditions, and customers. Price is important to the marketer because it is the only element of the marketing mix that generates revenue and profits rather than creating costs. It is also the most flexible marketing mix element, which marketers can change quickly to respond to changes in demand or the actions of competitors. Therefore, pricing strategy is a marketing technique that can be used to give the organization a competitive edge, and the key to success is to have a well-planned pricing strategy, establish pricing policies, and constantly monitor prices and operating costs to ensure adequate profits.

Factors Affecting Pricing Decisions

Planning for pricing decisions can be complex because a number of internal and external factors have to be considered. These factors are listed in Figure 7.1 and are discussed in the following paragraphs.

Learning Objectives

After reading this chapter, you should be able to

- define price,
- describe the internal and external factors that affect pricing decisions,
- explain the five main pricing methods,
- explain how the Internet is affecting pricing strategies,
- outline how to develop a pricing plan.

Internal Factors Affecting Pricing Decisions

Organizational and Marketing Objectives

Price needs to be consistent with organizational and marketing objectives. These objectives will vary in different organizations. Organizations requiring a rapid increase in market share will normally indulge in penetration pricing—charging low prices to capture a large share of the market and to discourage competitors from entering the market. On the other hand, organizations that seek high profits in the short term will set high prices. Such a practice is called price skimming. Other organizations may set their prices at par with the competition and decide to differentiate their products in other ways such as by offering better quality or service. Prices can be reduced if the marketing objective is to increase unit sales, for instance.

Pricing objectives can be classified into two categories:

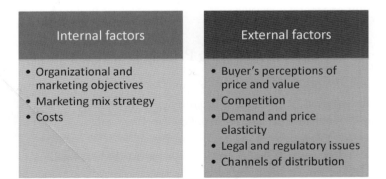

Internal factors	External factors
• Organizational and marketing objectives • Marketing mix strategy • Costs	• Buyer's perceptions of price and value • Competition • Demand and price elasticity • Legal and regulatory issues • Channels of distribution

Figure 7.1. Internal and external factors affecting pricing decisions.

1. *Quantitative objectives.* These include profits, sales, or market share maximization; market share increase; return on investment; coverage of existing capacity; price differentiation; cost coverage; return on assets; liquidity maintenance; price and sales stability in the market; and determination of fair prices for customers.

2. *Qualitative objectives.* These include long-term survival, service quality leadership, distributors' needs and satisfaction, price war avoidance, market development, barrier to entry for new competitors into the market, customers' needs and satisfaction, achievement of social goals, retention of existing customers, and so on.[2]

Marketing Mix Strategy

Price levels must not be determined in isolation from other marketing mix elements. Each element must be consistent with the others so that a cohesive mix is developed. A product with an "up-market" image and promotional campaign requires an appropriately high price rather than a discount price, as well as a select channel of distribution and selling program.

Costs

Variable costs of production, distribution, and marketing—such as labor, raw materials, and packaging costs—are those that vary with the volume of production. Fixed costs—such as equipment and machinery costs, rent, insurance, and property tax—are those that do not vary with production or sales levels. Total costs are variable and fixed costs added together.

Total costs = fixed costs + variable costs

In the short term, organizations may set prices that do not recover variable costs but only fixed costs. However, in the long run, the organization's survival will depend on the total costs being fully met for producing and selling an item.

External Factors Influencing Pricing Decisions

Buyers' Perceptions of Price and Value

As shown in chapter 4, where we discussed consumer buying behavior, different customers place different values on products they buy. Organizations must understand the importance that customers place on price, and this will vary according to the market and target segment. If customers perceive the price to be greater than the value they attach to a product, they will not make the purchase.

Competition

Pricing depends on the type of competition in the market. As shown in chapter 2 (see Figure 2.3), we can distinguish four types of competition, including monopoly, oligopoly, monopolistic competition, and pure competition.

A pure monopoly consists of only one seller. If it is a government monopoly,

- it might set a price below cost to make products accessible to people who cannot afford them,
- it might set the price to recover costs or at a level to generate good revenue,
- it might set a high price to reduce consumption.

Unregulated monopolies can set whatever prices they like. However, they might not always charge the highest price possible for fear of attracting government regulation or competition, or because they might want to penetrate the market by using a lower price. Regulated monopolies are usually allowed to set reasonable prices that will generate a fair return.

Oligopolists tend to price very close to each other. In this type of market, there are high barriers to entry, and a few sellers supply a homogeneous or a differentiated product, such as in the automobile or computer industry. If an organization reduces its price, buyers will switch to its products. Other organizations will respond by cutting their prices too, and this will result in a price war. Very little is gained through price cuts. On the other hand, if an organization increases its price, it may lose its customers if other oligopolists did not increase their prices.

In a monopolistic competition situation, many competitors are selling a product differentiated on the basis of physical characteristics, quality features, and brand images (e.g., airlines, soups, and breakfast cereals). Price can be used to differentiate offerings to customers, but most sellers are likely to practice nonprice competition to differentiate their products.

The pure competition markets consist of many sellers supplying homogeneous or uniform products, such as fruits and vegetables, cotton, and sugar. Organizations must sell their product at the going market price because they do not have influence on the market price. If a seller charges prices above the market price, customers will move to other sellers. If a seller reduces its price, customers will be attracted until other sellers reduce their prices too. A study revealed that retailers reacted to competitive entry and intensifying price competition by engaging in either price cuts or price increases.[3]

Demand and Price Elasticity

Setting different prices leads to different levels of demand. The relationship between the price charged and the demand level is mapped into a demand curve as shown in Figure 7.2 for normal products and for luxury products. For normal goods, it seems logical that as price goes up, demand falls, and conversely as price falls, demand rises. This is the standard demand curve that slopes downward. However, in the case of luxury goods—such as perfumes, some cars, and designer clothes—if the price

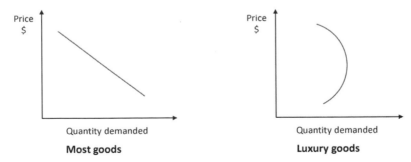

Figure 7.2. Demand curves for most goods and luxury goods.

goes up, people may tend to buy more of the good, and the demand curve is therefore upward sloping.

Marketers should also have some understanding of the price elasticity of demand—that is, the sensitivity of demand to price changes.

$$\text{Price elasticity of demand} = \frac{\% \text{ change in quantity demanded}}{\% \text{ change in price}}$$

Demand is considered price elastic when a small increase in price produces a large decrease in the quantity demanded. Here, price elasticity of demand is greater than 1. Total revenue falls because the extra income from the price rise does not fully compensate for the fall in demand. This is shown in Figure 7.3 where the revenue before the price increase was $P_1 \times Q_1$, and after the price increase, revenue falls to $P_2 \times Q_2$.

Conversely, a fall in price increases demand to the point where the total revenue rises. So when demand is elastic, sellers may prefer to increase their revenue by reducing prices. Usually buyers are more price sensitive when many substitutes are available for the product and when the price of the product represents a greater proportion of income.

In the case of price inelastic demand, revenue rises as price goes up as shown in Figure 7.4.

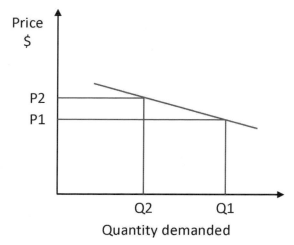

Figure 7.3. Price elastic demand.

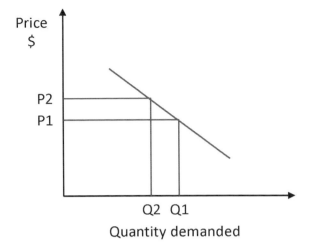

Figure 7.4. Price inelastic demand.

In such a case, the marketer may prefer to increase price to get more revenue.

Legal and Regulatory Issues

Pricing may be influenced to a large extent by governments and regulatory agencies such as the Competition and Consumer Commissions, which impose controls on prices. For example, the Australian Competition and Consumer Commission promotes fair trade and competition in the marketplace to protect consumers, businesses, and the community.[4] In the United States, the Federal Trade Commission protects American consumers.[5]

Channels of Distribution

The organization's pricing discretion may be eroded when it has to take into account the needs and expectations of other members of the distribution chain. Each will have a desired level of profit margin.

General Pricing Approaches

Marketers can use five main pricing approaches for setting purposeful and sound prices. They are cost-based, demand-based, competition-based, channel-based, and product mix-based approaches. These approaches take into account some of the key pricing issues discussed earlier. Any one main method of operation can be adopted, or a flexible combination can be used depending on the circumstance.

Cost-Based Methods

Cost-plus pricing and break-even analysis are two commonly used cost-oriented approaches to setting prices.

Cost-Plus Pricing or Mark-Up Pricing

Here, organizations add a predetermined percentage to the cost of their product to provide a profit margin. This method is most often adopted by retailers and wholesalers. Mark-ups can be expressed as a percentage of the cost or as a percentage of the selling price. Examples of mark-up pricing as a percentage of cost and selling price can be illustrated as follows.

A retailer purchases a bottle of whisky for \$300, adds \$150 to the cost, and then prices and sells the bottle of whisky at \$450:

$$\text{Mark up as a percentage of cost} = \frac{150}{300} = 50\%$$

$$\text{Mark up as a percentage of selling price} = \frac{150}{450} = 33\%$$

Cost-plus pricing is a simple method to use, and sellers can earn a fair return on their investment. However, this method only takes into account the internal costs of the organization and ignores external factors, such market demand and the actions of competitors.

Break-Even Analysis or Target Profit Pricing

The break-even analysis is a technique that shows the relationship between total revenue and total cost in order to determine the profitability of different levels of output. The break-even point (BEP) is the point at which total revenue and total costs are equal—no profit is made, nor are any losses incurred—as shown in Figure 7.5.

$$\text{Break-Even Point} = \frac{\text{Total Fixed Costs}}{\text{Unit Price} - \text{Variable Cost per Unit}}$$

From the BEP, we can easily calculate the lowest price that can be set, or a target price can be set, which will produce a particular level of profit. This pricing method focuses internally on cost structures and externally on a potentially simplistic relationship between price and sales. It ignores demand—organizations cannot be sure to sell x units at price y.

Demand-Based Pricing

The demand-based pricing approach is based on the level of demand for the product and therefore is customer-focused. When demand is strong, marketers will charge a high price, and when demand is weak, they will charge a low price. Therefore, the effectiveness of this method depends on the marketer's ability to estimate demand accurately. Assuming buyers value the product at levels sufficiently above the product's cost, demand-based pricing can enable an organization to reach higher profit levels.

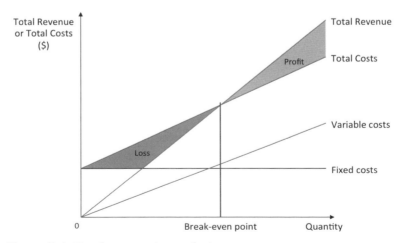

Figure 7.5. Break-even point analysis.

Competition-Based Pricing

This approach to setting prices is based on determining what competitors are pricing for similar or alternate products. Going-rate pricing is a competition-based approach where prices are fixed either above, below, or at the same level as competing brands. With sealed-bid or tender pricing, the organization bases its price on expectations of how competitors will price rather than on a rigid relation to the organization's costs or demand. Usually the organization that submits the lower price than competitors' wins the tender, but this is not always the case. Tenders can be judged on a value-for-money approach where organizations select winning tenders on the level of services that are supplied with the good—for example, a company purchasing a computer system may purchase a higher tender based on the level of after-sale service and technological support that is incorporated in the tender price.

Channel-Based Pricing

Intermediaries performing a number of functions on behalf of the supplier expect to be rewarded, and these rewards take the form of discounts against a nominal price list. Table 7.1 shows the types of discounts usually given.

Product-Mix-Based Pricing

Products are often bundled together and offered as one package. For example, a whale-watching cruise and hotel accommodation can be offered as a package to customers and usually the items cost more if bought separately. Table 7.2 illustrates some examples of product bundling.

Internet Pricing

Nowadays, global competition, e-commerce, and the Internet are affecting pricing decisions of organizations to a great extent. The Internet allows for dynamic, flexible, and real-time pricing, such as auction-type, group buying, or name-your-price pricing. The Internet has switched the power equation to the consumer who can now compare prices

Table 7.1. Channel-Based Pricing Approaches

Trade discounts
• Discount provided off the list price of the product to the retailer for performing additional services such as stockholding, redistribution, and so on.
Quantity discounts
• Reduced prices for large volume or bulk purchases.
Cash discounts
• Incentives given for purchasers to pay their bill quickly by offering discounts for early payment.
Promotional allowances
• Discount provided to intermediaries to help promote the product.
Geographical pricing
• Adjusting prices to account for the geographical location of customers, especially to reflect the costs of transport and insurance involved in getting the goods from buyer to seller. For example, free onboard pricing (FOB) means the goods are placed free onboard a carrier, and the buyer must pay for all transportation charges from the factory to the destination; cargo, insurance, freight pricing (CIF) means that the seller incurs all costs to the buyer's door.

from different organizations in one click of the mouse. Yet we see that many organizations selling their products and services online have not adopted dynamic pricing strategies. To maximize profits and create a competitive advantage, prices must be changed to reflect current market conditions.

Table 7.2. Product Bundling Pricing Approaches

Optional-product pricing
• Pricing-optional or accessory products sold with the main product (e.g., cars with and without power steering or alloy wheels)
Captive-product pricing
• Adding products that must be used with the main product (e.g., razor blades with razors or mobile phones with phone call plans and Internet access)
Product-bundle pricing
• Pricing bundles of products sold together at a reduced price (e.g., buy three for the price of two or gift boxes containing perfume and body lotion)

Developing a Pricing Plan

All the issues discussed earlier in this chapter have to be pulled together in order to prepare the pricing plan. The first step is to establish the pricing strategy of the organization.[6] For instance, does the organization want to charge a higher or lower price than the competition, or does it want to charge the same price as competitors?

With parity pricing or going-rate pricing, the organization will charge a price close to the competition and will use other forms of differentiation to differentiate its offerings, such as through product features and attributes, service, distribution channels, or guarantees.

Price skimming, or charging a higher price than competitors, is more appropriate when

- demand is price inelastic,
- there are different price-market segments with some buyers willing to pay a higher price than the rest of the market,
- there is little knowledge about the production and marketing costs.[7]

On the other hand, penetration pricing—setting a low price to increase sales and market share—is more relevant when

- demand is price elastic,
- competitors can enter the market quickly,
- there are no distinct price-market segments,
- high sales volume can lead to considerable savings in production and marketing costs.[8]

Nevertheless, when developing a pricing plan, the organization still has to be careful and consider all the other factors discussed here that influence pricing decisions.

The pricing plan will include questions and answers regarding the issues shown in Table 7.3.

Table 7.3. Summary of Questions to Be Asked to Set a Pricing Plan

Current position	• What is the current pricing decision based on (product, geography, segment, channel, etc.)? • Which allowances or discounts are currently being provided?

Aims and planned changes	• Where do you want to go?
	• Justify changes—are changes based on results, research, or competition?
	• What can be done?
	   • *Describe objectives.* These include market share, return on investment, profit level, position versus competition, and so on.
	   • *Describe factors influencing price setting.* These include costs, demand, price elasticity, stage of product life cycle, organizational objectives, competition, legal and economic considerations, and so on.
	   • *Choose the best pricing approach(s).* These include cost-based, demand-based, competition-based, or channel-based pricing, list price, discounts and allowances, and so on.

Action	• What resources and activities do you need to get there?
Start date and end date	

Summary

This chapter discussed the steps and factors to be taken into consideration when preparing a pricing plan. The organizational and marketing objectives, costs, and marketing mix elements are the internal factors that affect pricing decisions while customers' perceptions of price and value, type of competition in the market, demand and price elasticity, legal and regulatory issues, and channels of distribution are the external factors that influence pricing. The chapter also discussed five pricing methods, Internet pricing, and how to develop a pricing plan.

Chapter Review

1. Define and discuss the differences between demand elastic and demand inelastic pricing approaches. What are some examples of where you would use each approach (and justify your selections)?
2. Develop a break-even analysis for a manufacturing organization producing cans of gourmet beef stew for a total fixed cost per annum of $200,700, a current unit price of $2.95, and a variable cost per unit of $0.51 per can. What does this figure tell you in terms of profit or loss?
3. Considering the break-even analysis you just developed, if the organization wanted to ensure a target annual profit of $1.5 million, how many units per annum would it need to sell at the current price? How would this target figure change if the organization implemented a price skimming or a price penetration approach (assume that competing products' highest unit price is $3.95 and lowest unit price is $1.79)?
4. Discuss the differences between competition-based, demand-based and channel-based pricing approaches.
5. Considering the product-bundling approaches to pricing, provide two examples of real products for each approach and justify your choices. What are the benefits for organizations and for consumers of these pricing approaches?
6. Develop a pricing plan for a product of your choice. Include detailed justifications of the current position, aims and planned changes, and actions that must be taken.

CHAPTER 8

Planning for Integrated Marketing Communications

So what is integrated marketing communications or IMC? Having integrated marketing communications aims to ensure the consistency of the message and the complementary use of media. IMC requires the careful mixing of all marketing communication tools (the promotion mix elements), approaches, and resources within a company to provide a clear and distinct, coordinated message to target audiences. At the heart of marketing is communication—you can't sell something if you don't have a consumer to buy it, and you can't have a consumer unless you tell them about your company, your products and services, and the benefits of buying such products and services.

Learning Objectives

After reading this chapter, you should be able to

- understand the essential elements of the promotion mix,
- understand the importance and the necessity for having an integrated marketing communications plan,
- establish why organizational objectives are a key factor in developing an IMC plan,
- evaluate some of the baseline strategic elements required in developing an IMC plan.

The Promotion Mix Elements

The promotion mix elements are a set of tools that can be used for marketing communication purposes. The promotion mix elements include public relations, publicity, word of mouth, point of purchase (displays and packaging), advertising (print, television, radio, billboards, outdoor, and cinema, etc.); direct marketing (mail order and inbound and outbound telemarketing), online and interactive (websites, blogging, podcasts, wireless and mobile applications, e-mail, banners, Internet TV, and social networking); sales promotions; sponsorship and events; product placements (TV and movies); and personal selling. The main elements are shown in Figure 8.1.

Effective IMC planning means understanding the strengths and weaknesses of each of the promotion mix elements—understanding what each can and can't do on their own and how they can provide synergies when combined. Importantly, a good understanding of the IMC elements means understanding what they can do together as a whole.[1] An effective mix of the promotion tools must combine different elements to offset weaknesses and capitalize on strengths. Effective promotion is a result of a consistent message across all forms of communication. Table 8.1 provides a brief introduction to each of the elements, their uses, their strengths, and their weaknesses.[2]

Figure 8.1. The promotions mix elements.

Table 8.1. The Promotion Mix Elements: Definitions, Strengths, and Weaknesses

Element	Definition	Strengths	Weaknesses
Advertising	Nonpersonal, paid print (newspapers, magazines), and broadcast (TV, cinema, radio, outdoor) media communications.	Significant control over the message content, when and where it appears, and who is likely to view the message. Influences consumer perceptions, reminds, persuades, informs, and creates brand equity.	It is nonpersonal and often expensive to produce and distribute. There is a great deal of clutter so that messages may be missed or ignored. There is low credibility among target markets. It doesn't necessarily lead to sales.
Sales promotion	Short-term incentives to encourage purchase (discounts and free offers, product bundling, sampling, competitions, coupons, and loyalty programs).	Incentives can be provided to consumers and distribution network intermediaries to support product sales. Sales promotions create excitement and encourage immediate purchase.	There is a trade-off between short-term sales and long-term brand loyalty building. Again, there is a great deal of clutter that can make it hard to reach audiences.
Personal selling	Face-to-face or technology-mediated communications that can be one-to-one or one-to-many.	Direct contact provides the opportunity to meet consumer needs/wants and modify the offer accordingly. Gains immediate feedback on the offer.	High cost per individual consumer reached, and it may be difficult to ensure a consistent message. Sales people can have credibility issues—might require a great deal of relationship building over a long term.
Public relations (PR)	Usually directed at the corporate public (financial, internal, government, commercial suppliers, intermediaries, and general community) rather than individual customers; aims to develop long-term goodwill.	Can create and maintain customer loyalty, build pre-launch excitement, is very low cost, and has a potentially large impact with high credibility in the target market. Avoids advertising clutter.	It may be difficult for consumers to connect the product with the PR and may not result in transactions. It's difficult to measure the effectiveness, and messages may be inconsistent with other marketing communications.

Table 8.1. The Promotion Mix Elements: Definitions, Strengths, and Weaknesses (continued)

Element	Definition	Strengths	Weaknesses
Publicity	Nonpaid, editorial and mainstream media content—usually news or entertainment stories or pieces, such as press releases or press conferences provided to television, radio, and newspapers.	Editorial news stories are generally low or no cost and can be highly credible. Publicity also offers significant word-of-mouth communication potential.	There may be a significant lack of control over the message content, where or when it is transmitted, and who receives it. It can equally be negative or positive for the corporate image, as it may originate from outside the organization.
Online & interactive	Customized, direct communication that uses technology (Internet, e-mail, mobile phones) to deliver the message and encourage a response.	Responses are often immediate and measurable. The media informs, reminds, and persuades consumers, can attract attention, and is easily accessible. For business-to-business selling, the Internet is particularly useful to provide ordering (or reordering) services and extensive, specific, and individualized membership information and immediate feedback.	Clutter on the Internet is significant, slow connections or lack of connection can create issues, and SPAM (unsolicited e-mail or text messages) is a significant problem. Consumers can also be suspicious of purchasing on the Internet due to privacy concerns.
Direct marketing	Customized communications directly with target customers to generate a response or transaction. This uses direct-response media (direct mail, telemarketing, interactive TV, print, and Internet, etc.). It can be combined well with other promotion mix elements to good effect (incorporating database marketing activities).	Provides direct contact with large numbers of specifically targeted customers with limited waste coverage; can develop highly segmented markets with database mining capabilities. It's possible to build frequency into advertising and infomercial placement and lower costs.	Often has a negative image—junk mail; maintaining an accurate, up-to-date database can be difficult and costly. Appropriate content and mood creation of the editorial can be difficult, and printing and postage costs can be high.

Table 8.1. The Promotion Mix Elements: Definitions, Strengths, and Weaknesses (continued)

Element	Definition	Strengths	Weaknesses
Events & sponsorship	Supporting sporting, cultural, or social events, causes, and charities. This can be direct sponsorship and can provide naming rights with prominent logo and brand display.	Can be highly targeted (such as extreme sports or rock concerts) or can be more mainstream targeted (ads around football fields and on team jerseys); can use to support other relationship marketing activities (inviting high-level customers to sporting or cultural events); also used for internal marketing (staff attending sporting events).	Can be costly.
Product placements and branded entertainment	Product placement usually accounts for a small portion of ad budgets but is increasingly becoming popular (TV shows such as *Master Chef*, *My Kitchen Rules*, and *Top Gear* all have lots of product placement—product integration). Also includes content sponsorship, "advertainment," infomercials, and video on demand.	Exposure can be high and frequency can be high (video/DVD sales). Cost can be low; acceptance is often high. This type of advertising often bypasses regulations (e.g., alcohol and cigarettes can be prominently displayed) and cuts through clutter.	Can be high cost; no guarantee the target market will notice the brand; exposure times are limited; there's a limited appeal capacity, and lack of control over the message. There also can be clutter with significant competition for space.

Table 8.1. The Promotion Mix Elements: Definitions, Strengths, and Weaknesses (continued)

Element	Definition	Strengths	Weaknesses
Cinema	Advertisements shown prior to pre-views, ads in lobbies, signage, branding on food and drink packaging.	Has high exposure rates; consumer reac-tions to the film can influence percep-tions to the products advertised. Ad recall is usually good, and there is a lack of clutter. Cinema audiences are very well segmented, so ads reach well-defined target markets.	Audience irritation at the interruption; cost can be high for production and distribution.
Point of purchase and packaging (POP)	In-store media, such as ads, aisle displays, brochures, signage on aisles and shopping carts, in-store TV and radio broadcasts, and product packaging.	High consumer at-tention and influence on the purchase decision—affects impulse buying and can modify habitual purchasing behavior. It reaches consumers where and when the decision is made. POP displays can encour-age retailers to stock products prominently.	There are no real downsides to POP and packaging, although excessive displays can become costly and consumers may tend to ignore much of the signage unless it is specifically relevant.
Word of mouth (WOM)	Consumers often seek advice from peer networks or opinion leaders (trendset-ters, loyal customers) regarding products and brands.	High consumer atten-tion and influence on the purchase decision; can generate buzz and excitement around campaigns and prod-ucts with consumers themselves spreading the messages between peer networks.	It is difficult to iden-tify opinion leaders and target messages specifically to them. WOM also can be difficult to generate and control and can equally be negative (people tend to talk more to friends and family about negative experiences than they do about posi-tive ones). Negative WOM can spread rapidly with use of the Internet.

Determining the IMC Mix

Integrated marketing communications coordinate a company's outgoing message between different media and ensure the consistency of the message throughout. IMC is an aggressive marketing plan that captures and uses an extensive amount of customer information in setting and tracking marketing strategy, ensuring all forms of communications and messages are carefully linked together. Organizations cannot afford to rely on a single method or strategy to gain the required financial outcomes. On a global basis, with businesses starting up daily, a multitude of marketing methods are available from simple stand-alone billboards to multilingual websites. Therefore, designing a marketing plan that will encompass varying forms of integrated communication to consumers is paramount to the success of any product.

IMC decisions are concerned with the planning, implementation, and control of persuasive, integrated communications with target customers[3] to ensure that the right customers receive the right messages at the right times and in locations where they are receptive to those messages. The key here is strategic matching of specific communications to clearly defined target markets. For example, to sell surf-branded clothing and accessories to Generation Y consumers, it would not be appropriate to place infomercials on TV at midday. This would be a serious waste of scarce resources. A much better campaign is to have sponsorships of surfing events, spokespeople who are surfers wearing clothing items, and communicating using targeted websites and social networking websites.

IMC strategies should outline the types of activities proposed in relation to the goods and services provided, identify some of the strong selling points of the organization, be directed to the identified audience, be original in marketing, and keep the message simple. Most importantly, you should make certain the products presented represent what can be delivered. A number of factors affect IMC decisions, as shown in Figure 8.2.[4]

Figure 8.2. Factors affecting IMC decisions.

Product Factors

The type of product, its uses, and how, where, and when it is bought and consumed will all impact the IMC elements used.[5] For example, low-involvement, nondurable, fast-moving consumer goods that may be habitually purchased (such as breakfast cereal) will usually adopt a mass communication strategy using advertising and online marketing, point-of-purchase displays, and prominent packaging. However, for business-to-business products (particularly those with high degrees of technical specifications and a significant after-sale service component) personal selling will generate the best return on investment.

Demand and Supply Factors

Effective promotions activities will also need to consider demand and supply factors, such as the number of players in the industry, how strong the competitors are, and if there are many direct and indirect substitutions available (or only very few). The stage of the product life cycle will also affect the communication types and intensity. For example, the introductory stage requires a great deal of promotion (advertising, sales promotions, direct marketing, online marketing, personal selling, etc.) to inform and persuade consumers and sales promotions to obtain product trials. The growth stage shows increasing demand for the product and will require a greater emphasis on advertising to remind consumers of the product's benefits and availability. During the maturity stage, various forms of communication will be required but usually more periodically. Sales promotions will again become important, perhaps even creating new or updated POP and packaging. Direct and database marketing may also be more pertinent as consumer loyalty programs are developed to retain high-yield customers.

Elasticity of demand also plays a significant factor in developing IMC programs. Where demand is elastic—where changes in pricing will greatly affect demand for products such as luxury goods, entertainment, and vacations—higher prices may require more promotion activities to offset the lowered demand. Where demand is inelastic—when changes in prices do not greatly affect demand for products, such as for milk and bread, electricity, water, and gas—there is reduced need to develop advertising campaigns. (For further discussion on the elasticity of demand see chapter 6.)

Customer Factors

The major customer factors that affect IMC decisions are the differences in buyer behavior between business markets and consumer markets. In consumer markets (as discussed in chapter 3), consumers are influenced by personal, social, and psychological factors and may have any one or a variety of roles in the buying decision (initiator, influencer, decider, buyer, and user). Business markets (such as trade or industrial markets, government markets, institutional markets, and reseller markets) often have a much more formal decision-making processes, are generally fewer in number than consumer market audiences, usually purchase on a larger scale, might be geographically concentrated in a particular region (e.g., mining companies), and often demand close supplier-customer relationships. Business markets also have different decision-making roles in the buying process including users (members of organizations that use the

goods and services), influencers (those who often help to define specifications and provide information on alternatives), buyers (those who have
formal authority to purchase), deciders (those who might have formal or
informal power in the decision-making process and might be composed
of a committee), and gatekeepers (those who control the flow of information and access to others).[6]

The buyer roles for consumer markets and business markets will
influence the promotion mix element selection, as will the geographic
concentration and the number of consumers or businesses in the markets. If markets are very small in number and geographically located in
a small area, then personal (door-to-door) selling and direct marketing
strategies, such as database marketing, will be more useful. Where markets are geographically dispersed, and markets are large, then advertising,
outdoor, cinema, online, and interactive marketing, as well as some direct
marketing strategies, may be warranted. Public relations, events and
sponsorships, and WOM are often developed for business markets, while
sales promotions and publicity tend to have greater impact for consumer
markets.

Budget Factors

In a perfect world the promotions budget would be set based on the tasks
to be accomplished and the outcomes required. However, organizations
do not often operate in a perfect world, and there usually seems to be
fewer marketing dollars available than needed—regardless of the budgeting approach taken. Budgets may be set from the top management down,
where management sets the spending limits usually based on an arbitrary
allocation of funds, or from the bottom up, where promotion strategies
are developed and appropriate budgets are allocated based on the costs of
promotion activities.[7]

There are several ways to set promotion and advertising budgets, most
of which are based on economic reasons or as a response to sales or revenue.[8] For example, the simplest budget methods are the task method,
allocating the budget based on the tasks to be performed that align with
marketing objectives, and the percentage-of-sales method, allocating a
marketing budget total based on a target percentage of sales revenue.[9] The
next step up in the budget ladder is the competitive method, estimating

marketing budgets of leading competitors and using those estimates as a benchmark for your organization's expenditure targets. A more sophisticated budget method includes the marginal analysis process, which sets promotion budgets based on sales—when sales increase, then promotion budgets also increase, and when sales level off so too does the expenditure on promotion.

Sales- and revenue-based budgets, however, assume that sales are a direct response to, and measure of, advertising and promotion activity.[10] However, as shown in the strengths and weaknesses of mix elements in Table 8.1, only a few of the promotion mix elements will typically lead to a direct, measurable response from consumers. Budget also has to be available for brand development, corporate image marketing objectives, PR and publicity, sponsorship, and cause marketing activities to develop goodwill and community acceptance over the long term.

Marketing Mix Factors

Promotion decisions must not be made without due consideration of the other marketing mix elements. For example, the price and quality of the product and the brand life-cycle stage in relation to competing products must be considered when developing the promotion mix. Higher or lower prices should be supported by consumer perceptions of the relative (higher or lower) quality of the items and should be associated with promotion activities that demonstrate the quality level and justify the price.[11]

The choice of promotion mix elements will also be influenced by where and how the products are distributed. For example, if the distribution chain has only one level (manufacturer direct to consumers, as in the case of most services, such as restaurants and hair salons), then manufacturers can use promotion elements designed to specifically target end consumers (such as advertising, sales personnel, and direct marketing through database mining and relationship marketing programs). Whereas, for multilevel distribution channels that incorporate wholesalers and retailers as distribution points, then trade marketing can be used to communicate with intermediaries, and advertising can be used to again target end consumers—to create both push and pull strategies and move products through the channels as shown in Figure 8.3.

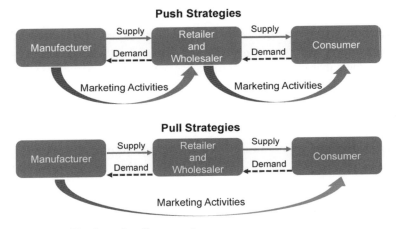

Figure 8.3. Push and pull strategies.

As manufacturers become further removed from end consumers with more intermediaries involved in the channel, there will need to be a greater emphasis on integrated promotion and communication campaigns to ensure that all channel members and end consumers are educated on the product's benefits and features. Further emphasis also will be placed on sales promotion activities (for both end consumers and channel intermediaries), and sales staff and other internal audiences will also require promotion campaigns.

IMC Strategy Development

Understanding your customer is the first rule of any business operation. Therefore in developing IMC strategies, it is critical to the success of the plan that marketers are fully aware of client needs, wants, and desires. Customers want the benefits that a company has to offer, not necessarily the goods and services delivered. For example, when consumers buy mouthwash, some want it for the refreshing taste and fresh breath, some consumers are buying it for protection from gum disease, and yet others are buying it for whiter teeth. This is where a strong understanding of the organization's consumer base will provide the required elements in establishing effective IMC strategies. Added to this, we must also remember to plan the links across all promotion mix elements. We need to ensure that we have a consistent message with coherent images and text or copy, and we need to plan for the synergies between the elements.

Once specific, measurable, achievable, realistic, and time- bound (SMART) marketing objectives have been set, effective IMC strategies can then be developed based on our knowledge and understanding of our target consumers. For each marketing objective, we need to ask the **4WHEBA** questions: *Who*; *What*; *Where*; *When*; *How*; how we will *Evaluate* the outcomes from the program; how we will develop a *Budget*; and who will take responsibility for the *Actions*. These questions are summarized in Table 8.2.[12]

Table 8.2. Summary of Questions to Be Asked to Set IMC Strategies

Who	Who is/are the target audience(s)? What is their current stage of buyer readiness? What do they know about us and our products? What do they know or believe about our competitors? What are their demographic, psychographic, behavioral, and geographic characteristics?
What	What response is sought from the target audience(s)? Do we want brand recognition, sales, feedback, website visits, and so on? What do we want consumers to say, feel, believe, understand, or know about our products, brands, or organization? What do we *not* want consumers to think, say, feel, believe, and so on?
Where	Where are consumers most likely to purchase products? For example, if your organization is operating storefronts, do those stores have specific opening hours, nine to five perhaps, or do those storefronts provide a benefit to customers who only shop during weekend and evening hours? Can you extend trading hours or locations (develop a website perhaps)? Where are the most cost-effective places for consumers to view our communication messages? For example, which media vehicle— newspapers, TV, radio, billboards, POP, Internet, cinema, magazines, and so on—will reach them? Ideally, multiple locations are going to be needed to ensure that you reach a number of market segments.
When	When will messages be displayed, and what is the justification for the scheduling? For example, Christmas messages are best scheduled from October to December, back-to-school messages in July, Easter messages in March and April, and so on. Scheduling may also relate to stage of the product life cycle or quadrant of the Boston Consulting Group (BCG) matrix. For example, intensive scheduling may be warranted for products in the introduction or growth stages of the PLC or for star products on the BCG matrix, while products in the maturity stage or cash cow products may only require periodic scheduling for a 2–3 week block every 6–8 months. Again, ideally organizations should aim for multiple time slots to pick up different target markets.
How	How will our communication messages be best developed/displayed? How will the message best appeal to the target audience (e.g., slice of life, cartoons, jingles, testimonials, scientific evidence, fantasy)? Can we use a rational appeal, an emotional appeal, a moral appeal, or some combination of these?

Table 8.2. Summary of Questions to Be Asked to Set IMC Strategies (continued)

Evaluation and measurement	What results do we expect, and how will we measure these for return on investment? If we intend to measure results, what do we need to do prior to the campaign running? For example, take a count of stock on hand, run a sales promotion, and then determine the profitability of the promotion activity based on remaining stock or on receipts. How will we evaluate the success of the communication program?
Budget	Set the budget and determine the level of resources for the activities. Determine how expenditure will be controlled.
Action	Who (department or individual) is to do what and when to develop the programs?

Summary

Effective IMC strategies will determine where the organization's product(s) fit into the competitive marketplace. The key to developing successful IMC programs is to ensure clear and specific links with SMART marketing objectives and—moving further up the strategic hierarchy—ultimately the corporate objectives. Marketing objectives highlight the tie between products and the marketplaces, while IMC strategies provide a means by which the objectives will be attained. Formulation of IMC strategies will be dependent on the organization itself, size, diversity, finances, and mission, as well as the other elements of the marketing mix, the product and its relative price and quality, demand and supply factors, budget factors, and the consumers. IMC programs will also need to take account of push strategies—pushing the products through the channel—and pull strategies—using demand to pull products through the channel.

In developing an IMC plan, it is important to remember that any long-term strategies must work in harmony with other short-term operational planning. Marketers need to know their customers, the strengths of the organization, and be able to sell the organization's benefits. IMC development should take into account changes to the marketplace over time, requiring flexibility to adjust the program if expected results are not being met. IMC development needs to also consider the product lifecycle stage and BCG matrix quadrants.

Chapter Review

1. The lead into the chapter talks about what IMC is and the various promotions elements or tools that may be used to communicate a message. Given the variety of elements available, if you were the head of marketing for an organization and you had to evaluate and possibly redesign the organization's brand campaign, summarize each of the elements available and their potential strengths and weaknesses.

2. Most companies run ad-hoc marketing plans; they market on the fly as required. As the marketing director, what approaches would you take to set promotion strategies for a more effective communication campaign?

3. As a marketing manager for a medium-sized pharmaceutical company, your CEO has a marketing philosophy of shooting from the hip, based on the fact that he or she has a background in finance and little knowledge about marketing strategies. What strategies would you employ to provide the CEO and the rest of the organization staff with a better understanding of where marketing can contribute to the overall profitability and longevity of the organization?

4. You and two friends have just started a new urban wear clothing company. How will you go about putting together an IMC campaign?

5. How would you explain push and pull strategies?

6. What are the 4WHEBA questions that guide the development of successful IMC strategies?

7. You have been working for the same company for the past five years, sales are good, not great, but the company is making a small profit. You have developed industry networks, conducted industry research, and used a variety of low-level relationship marketing techniques (you have developed a card file listing of a number of your large customers). A new boss has been hired and believes that the status quo is not enough and wants to lift the organization's game. How will you go about creating, modifying, or altering your current IMC processes given your past five years of status quo with somewhat positive results?

CHAPTER 9

Planning for Distribution Channels and Market Logistics

Distribution channels and logistics planning, sometimes called place in marketing, is concerned with getting the right products to the right customers, at the right price, at the right place, and at the right time. Therefore, planning for distribution and logistics is concerned with delivering value to end consumers. Traditionally, organizations have supply chains—the upstream organizations—that constitute the networks of suppliers that provide raw materials, services, and other activities necessary to feed into the process to develop products for end users. Added to this, organizations have distribution channels—the downstream intermediaries—that link manufacturers with end consumers. Products are moved through the supply chains and distribution channels from manufacturers to end users through a process of logistics management. Each party involved in the total marketing value chain can create and add value along the chain.

Channels and logistics planning are interwoven with other marketing functions and marketing mix elements, such as product, price, and promotion. Marketing value chain management should be integrated with the marketing concept, market orientation, and relationship marketing to achieve differential advantage.[1] Since channel and logistics management is a major cost factor of a product, it can be a means to achieve a competitive advantage by lowering the costs to accomplish a cost leadership strategy or by providing superior service to customers to attain a differentiation advantage. As with other marketing mix elements, distribution channel and market logistics planning should be based on internal, external, and target market analyzes.

Learning Objectives

After studying this chapter, you will be able to

- understand the issues of the marketing value chain management,
- appreciate various channels levels and intermediaries,
- discuss what is involved in channel planning,
- identify the market logistics issues.

Marketing Value Chain Management

A marketing value chain is a series of activities involving all members—directly or indirectly—to procure materials, process the materials, and distribute the finished products with an aim to fulfilling customers' needs. In general, marketers are concerned with two major elements in the marketing value chain management: the distribution channel and logistics management. Value chain members include suppliers, wholesalers, retailers, transporters, and other participants, such as customers. Figure 9.1 shows a typical manufacturer's marketing value chain.

As previously mentioned, the marketing value chain is a reflection of the fact that parties can add value to the product throughout the chain.

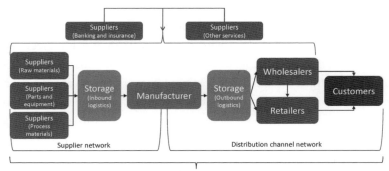

Figure 9.1. The marketing value chain.

Typically, not only do the firms manage their own operations and immediate suppliers, but they also manage the immediate suppliers' supply chains. There are a number of driving forces for this change.

- *The customer driving force.* Customers are more informed and empowered because of the availability of information from the Internet and other sources. It is very easy for customers to compare prices, product attributes, and warranties, among other factors. Customers are equipped with ample information that can help them to make a purchase decision. Changing demographics such as single-parent households and two-career families have forced customers to be more time conscious and demanding. As a result, marketers need to provide customers with products that offer better value, more competitive prices, greater convenience, flexibility, higher quality, and faster responses.

- *The technology driving force.* Not only does technology provide customers with vital information, but it also affects how they purchase products. Traditionally, marketers dictated where and when customers could buy their products. The availability of technology has changed this behavior. Information technology provides a means for customers to purchase products at their own time and place. For example, airline tickets can be bought online instead of from a travel agent. Customers can order customized computers on the Internet.

- *The supply chain driving force.* In the past, manufacturers were in a dominant position over channel intermediaries with the capability to dictate marketing practices. However, the bargaining power of intermediaries, especially retailers, has increased significantly in recent years. With mergers and acquisitions that consolidate the number of retailers and the backward integration strategy of retailers to introduce private label products, retailers have been able to gain greater bargaining power.

- *The globalization driving force.* The phenomenon of globalization is the result of increasing the similarity of markets around the globe.[2] This similarity was caused by improved communications, travel, and the convergent tastes of similar segments in different countries. The impact of technology—which has revolutionized communications, especially in media—enables people in even the most isolated places to gain knowledge of, and to understand the culture of, others and to acquire information about the latest products, features, and brands. The wide availability of affordable transportation allows consumers to travel between cities, across national borders, and between continents. Knowledge, innovation, and experience have created the demand for more advanced and sophisticated products. Consumers can choose products and intermediaries from all over the world rather than limit their options to domestic areas. Globalization makes the marketing value chain more complex because more and unfamiliar intermediaries are involved in business transactions.

The implications of these driving forces indicate that marketers need to take a holistic and proactive approach to manage their channel and logistics issues. When making channel and logistics policies and strategies, marketers need to consider the issues related not only to their own operations but also to those of their intermediaries as well. In addition, futuristic thinking to anticipate the potential opportunities and threats that are associated with the marketing value chain activities should be factored into the planning process.

Planning for Distribution Channels

A distribution channel is a set of people and firms that facilitates the flow of a product from manufacturer to end user. Three major parties are involved in a distribution channels: manufacturers, end users, and intermediaries. An intermediary is an independent person or firm that operates in between the manufacturer and the end user. Intermediaries sometimes are called resellers, middlemen, or jobbers. In addition to buying and selling the manufacturers' products, they also perform other marketing activities such as personal selling, promoting, and gathering market intelligence. Intermediaries may or may not take the title of the goods in transit from the manufacturer to the end users.

The Importance of Intermediaries

Intermediaries are an important party in an exchange process. In general, they perform a number of functions between the manufacturers and end users.

Transactional Functions

Intermediaries act as buying agents for customers. They buy for end users and sell for manufacturers. In order to perform the buying function, they need to understand customers' needs and have good knowledge of the market. With regard to the selling function, intermediaries require marketing and selling capabilities, such as conducting sales promotion, setting prices, and managing a strong and efficient sales force.

Physical Functions

Intermediaries facilitate exchanges between manufacturers and customers, providing warehousing services to both customers and manufacturers. They perform the storing function so that manufacturers can deliver the products to intermediaries in bulk and customers can buy the quantity they want at a particular time. Efficient storing can reduce inventory risks and costs for both manufacturers and customers.

As mentioned in the storing function, intermediaries can buy in bulk from manufacturers and repack the products in smaller quantities to suit different types of customers—sorting and dividing the products. Intermediaries may buy from different manufacturers and form an assortment to ship to customers.

Intermediaries also provide regular delivery to customers—transporting products—reducing the manufacturers' risks and freight costs by buying in bulk and carrying stocks in intermediaries' warehouses.

Facilitating Functions

By providing customers with credit and assisting with customer financing, intermediaries reduce the customers' pressure on capital requirements.

Smaller retailers often rely on financial credit from intermediaries to run businesses or even to survive.

Intermediaries can also collect and disseminate market intelligence about competitors' activities, new product developments, customers' tastes, and retailers' movements.

Designing Distribution Channels

There are four major decisions when designing distribution channels: determining the types of channels, determining the intensity of distribution, determining which specific intermediaries to use, and determining how to motivate intermediaries.

Determining the Types of Channel

The first decision marketers need to make is what types of intermediaries they can use. The simplest approach is the *direct* distribution channel. That is, manufacturers get their products directly to the end users. No intermediaries are involved in the transaction, and this is considered to be a zero channel arrangement. Examples of firms using the direct distribution channel are Dell, Avon, Encyclopedia Britannica, and mail-order houses. Contrary to the direct distribution channel, *indirect* distribution channels involve at least one intermediary. It can be a retailer or a wholesaler and a retailer.

When indirect distribution is adopted, marketers must decide the type(s) of intermediaries that best suit their firms. The types of intermediaries may be a discount store, a specialty retailer, a grocery store, or a specialized wholesaler. The use of one type of intermediary may affect another type to work with the firms in the distribution channel.

Instead of using one type of intermediary, marketers can adopt a multiple channel distribution, which is sometimes called hybrid or dual distribution. A multiple channel approach offers the same brand or line of products through a variety of different intermediaries to the same target market. For example, publishers sell their novels through specialty stores and discount stores and online as e-books.

Determining the Intensity of Distribution

Distribution intensity is "the number of intermediaries used by a manufacturer at the retail and wholesale levels in a particular territory."[3] Distribution coverage can range from narrow coverage to widespread coverage. Narrow coverage can be in the form of exclusive distribution or selective distribution, and intensive distribution is widespread distribution as shown in Figure 9.2.

Intensive distribution. With intensive distribution, manufacturers endeavor to sell their products through as many intermediaries of a particular type as possible. Manufacturers of fast-moving consumer goods such as bread, soft drinks, biscuits, and shampoos often use intensive distribution. The advantages of this type of distribution are increased sales volume, wide consumer recognition, low unit costs, and considerable impulse purchasing. Disadvantages include low price, low margin, small order sizes, and difficulty obtaining support from intermediaries.

Selective distribution. Manufacturers choose a small number of intermediaries to handle the organization's brands or product lines. This approach is especially suitable for products such as household appliances and consumer electronics. The reason is that customers are willing to

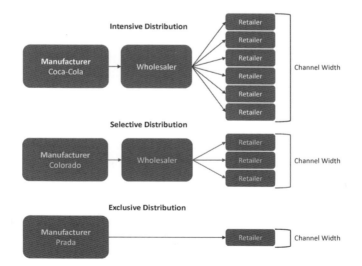

Figure 9.2. Determining the intensity of distribution.

spend more time to compare options at the retail level. The major advantages of selective distribution are enhancement of the image of a brand, strengthening of customer service, improvement of quality control, and maintenance of some influence of price setting.[4]

Exclusive distribution. This approach sells a product line or brand only through an intermediary in a specific geographic area. Rolex watches and expensive yachts are examples of manufacturers adopting this approach. Manufacturers usually expect their exclusive intermediaries not to carry competing brands. Since the success of manufacturers and intermediaries rely on each other, both parties need to work closely to ensure that the set objectives and marketing strategies are understood and carried out. While some market coverage may be sacrificed with this approach, it has a few advantages. The brand image can be enhanced with limited retailers carrying the brand. Exclusive intermediaries are also more likely to be motivated to push the brand, as they usually earn a higher margin or receive a higher commission rate.

Determining Which Specific Intermediaries to Use

Once the decisions of the types and the density of the distribution have been made, marketers' attention should be focused on the selection of the specific intermediaries. The manufacturers must examine closely the potential intermediaries that can best provide their marketing efforts and best fit the firms' total marketing strategies. Criteria to evaluate the suitability of potential intermediaries include their financial, human, and physical resources;[5] experience; and reputation in the industry. Financial resources that need to be evaluated are revenue, profit and loss, balance sheets, number of sales agents, sales performance of related product lines, and general sales performance. Human resources includes an organization's management strength in planning, its relationship with employees, its strategic direction, its training programs, and its technical competence. Physical resources consist of the plant, equipment, inventory and warehousing facilities, and ordering and payment procedures.

Experience can be evaluated in terms of years in the business, market coverage, and past marketing and selling programs. Issues with regard to reputation are the leadership, establishment, community standing, ethics, background of key executives, willingness to cooperate with manufacturers and share information, and level of expertise.

Determining How to Motivate Intermediaries

The marketers' job in distribution channel management is not finished after selecting the most suitable channel members. They need to motivate intermediaries to perform well. Motivation is a complicated issue because it involves cooperation and conflict.[6] Because of the interdependency between manufacturers and intermediaries, they need some form of cooperation and coordination of activities.[7] This cooperation and coordination is important in order to maintain a predictable and dependable relationship between the parties. With the purpose of fostering cooperation and reducing conflict with the intermediaries, marketers should attempt to understand the needs of their intermediaries. Some intermediaries might need more intensive training, while others might consider heavy promotion necessary to push the products. These differences exemplify the importance of understanding and evaluating the intermediaries' willingness to cooperate in step three of designing distribution channels. In general, marketers can use financial rewards, nonfinancial rewards, or both to motivate channel intermediaries. In China, for example, the provision of appropriate incentives and boosting staff training are considered as two critical elements in motivating distribution channel members.[8] While financial rewards can be in the forms of dealer contests, financial deals, cooperative promotion, and sales aids, nonfinancial rewards can contain the provision of new products, training, technical support, and recognition awards.

Planning for Logistics

Logistics is "the process of anticipating customer needs and wants; acquiring the capital, materials, people, technologies, and information necessary to meet those needs and wants; optimizing the goods—or service-producing network to fulfill customer requests; and utilizing the network to fulfill customer requests in a timely way."[9]

Market logistics is concerned with the efficient and effective physical delivery of products valued by the customers. Market logistics is able to provide marketers with a competitive advantage in contemporary marketing. Two main factors contribute to this situation. First, market orientation instead of product or production orientation has driven organizations to focus more on customer services to satisfy their wants. Marketers recognize that market logistics is one of the marketing tools that can offer target customers with better services. It, thus, has become a strategic focus and has gained recognition. The second factor is concerned with costs. Rising transportation and inventory maintenance costs have driven marketers to look for ways of controlling costs. With the assistance of technology and automation, logistics is an area that can improve productivity. Organizations are more willing to commit resources, as efficiency can be achieved and measured relatively easily.

There are six main functions in planning for market logistics:

1. Order processing
2. Warehousing
3. Inventory management
4. Materials handling
5. Packaging and unitization
6. Transportation[10]

Order Processing

Order processing concerns the receipt, handling, and filling of orders. A customer's order initiates the physical distribution process. The order processing function usually involves checking customer credit, granting credit, transferring information to sales records, transmitting the order to the inventory and shipping areas, preparing shipping documents, and collecting past-due accounts. Marketers need to design an order-processing flow that covers all these activities in a systematic manner. Coordination between the sales and other departments is critical, as these activities usually involve more than one department.

Accuracy, reliability, and speed are crucial in order processing. Sales departments, once orders are received, should check all the details of the orders and pass them on to other concerned departments to facilitate the delivery of the orders as soon as possible. Electronic order systems can be used to facilitate accurate, reliable, and speedy order processing. Meeting

delivery dates is one of the major factors in a buyer's choice of manufacturer because it can help intermediaries manage their inventories.
Thus accurate, reliable, and speedy processing can become a competitive
advantage for manufacturers.

Warehousing

Warehousing is for the keeping of products until they are physically
moved to another place. Warehousing marketers need to make two prominent decisions: the type and number of warehouses and the location of
warehousing. Two types of warehouses are available to marketers: private
(firm-owned) warehouses and public (independently owned) warehouses.
Advantages of a private warehouse include greater flexibility in design to
satisfy special storage and handling requirements, greater control over the
warehouse facility and its operations, lower unit costs if a large volume of
products are involved, and better ability to handle seasonal fluctuations
of demand. A public warehouse, in contrast, does not require a fixed initial investment by the firms and offers location flexibility, the ability to
increase warehouse space to handle unexpected orders, and lower costs if
the volume of an order is small.

The decision for the number and location of warehouses is related to
the customer service level set by the organization and the distance between
supply sources and markets. In general, fewer warehouses are required
when customer service levels are lower, supply sources and markets are
closely located, or both. There is a trade-off relationship between the
customer service level and the number of warehouses. The warehousing
cost rises with greater numbers of warehouses. However, the organization can enhance customer service levels by shortening the delivery lead
times.

Inventory Management

The aim of inventory management is to keep the inventory cost as low
as possible while maintaining a specified customer service level. The two
major inventory management decisions are how much to order and when
to reorder. Both decisions are based on the organization's sales forecasts.
As with as warehousing management, a specified customer service level is

an important factor to consider in inventory management. While some intermediaries may give the manufacturers a longer period to deliver orders, some would ask for immediate delivery or place orders with short delivery times. Marketers need to thoroughly understand the expectations of various intermediaries and respond to differences in the expected levels of customer service.

How Much to Order

Marketers can use the economic order quantity (EOQ) method to determine how much inventory to order each time to minimize total costs. The total inventory cost consists of order-processing cost and inventory-carrying cost. When these two costs are at an equilibrium, the total inventory costs are at a minimum. That signifies the EOQ point.

Order-processing cost is the cost of placing, preparing, and processing an order. The order-processing cost per unit of product decreases as the order quantity increases. The reason is that order-processing cost is a fixed cost, which can be spread over a larger number of ordered units.

Inventory-carrying cost contains costs of storage, handling, damages, insurance, and record keeping. Contrary to the order-processing cost, the inventory-carrying cost per unit increases as the order quantity increases. The reason is that the finished products will stay in inventory longer as the order quantity increases.

Figure 9.3 shows the relationships between order-processing cost, inventory-carrying cost, and total cost.

The formula for calculation of EOQ is as follows:

$$EOQ = \sqrt{2ra \div i},$$

where r = the annual rate of demand for the product in units, a = the cost of placing an order ($ per order), and i = the cost of holding one unit of product for one year.

To illustrate how the EOQ can be applied in practice, assume that ABC Company sells TV sets that it buys from a supplier for $60 each. The demand for these TV sets is constant at 50 per month—that is, 600 per year. The order-processing cost is $30 and the inventory-carrying cost is $10 per annum. Assuming that there are no stock-outs and the lead time for replenishment is zero, EOQ can be calculated as follows:

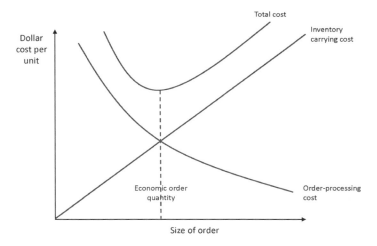

Figure 9.3. Economic order quantity and the relationships between order-processing cost, inventory-carrying cost, and total cost.

$$EOQ = \sqrt{2ra} \div i,$$

where r = 600 units, a = $30, and i = $10.

$$EOQ = \sqrt{(2)\ (600)\ (30)} \div 10$$

$$= \sqrt{3,600} \div 10$$

$$= 60 \text{ units per order.}$$

Therefore, an order of 60 TV sets is the optimal—that has the lowest total cost.

Materials Handling

Materials handling is concerned with the internal movement and flow of raw materials, semifinished goods, and finished goods from receipt to dispatch at the facility's premises. Successful materials handling contributes toward improving manufacturing operations, increasing effective capacity, developing effective working conditions, reducing heavy labor, improving logistics service, and reducing costs. The type of products to be handled affects what material handling system to use. For example, handling bulky products, such as cement and raw sugar, is very different from handling finished products, such as cosmetics and soaps.

Marketers need to consider three dimensions of materials handling: movement, time, and space.

1. *Movement.* This dimension involves the transference of goods into, within, and out of warehouses in an efficient manner.
2. *Time.* This dimension is concerned with getting raw materials ready for production or finished goods ready for customer order delivery. Efficient materials handling can lessen the time to get raw materials to production, reducing the chances of work stoppage, an accumulation of higher inventories, and a holding of bigger storage spaces. Similarly, the shorter time it takes to convey the finished goods to the shipping area, the shorter the order cycle time and the higher the level of perceived customer service.
3. *Space.* The space in warehouses is fixed, and materials handling equipment occupies space. Materials handling equipment needs to be utilized in an effective manner. For example, a turret truck can be used in a narrow aisle to lift a pallet of goods.

   Firms can use mechanical and automated equipment to handle materials. Mechanical equipment is a combination of labor and handling equipment, while automated equipment endeavors to minimize the labor involved to lower the labor cost.

   An efficient and effective way to handle materials is containerization, which is to deliver a shipment of products in a sealed container. Containerization minimizes physical handling of the products. As a result, it reduces damage, lessening the risk of theft and allowing for more efficient transportation.[11]
4. *Packaging and unitization.* From the logistics perspective, packaging and unitization address the issues of arranging products in proper units for storing, handling, and transferring. A product's physical form and nature will influence what kind of packaging is needed to contain it. For instance, food products would need a packaging of food grade—that is, a nonpoisonous grade of material. The size and shape of packaging should aim to optimize the space utilization during storage and during transport. The dimensions of packaging should take into consideration possible packing arrangements in a shipping container, pallet patterns, and space utilization.

In addition to containerization as mentioned in the materials handling section, palletization and bulk packaging are two other major considerations. A pallet is a flat, rectangular structure on which a number of small units of product can be stacked, so they can be transported and stored in a stable manner by mechanical means.[12] The pallet pattern is the collection of units of products on a pallet and can affect storage efficiency, distribution systems, and compact loading.

Bulk packaging is commonly used for the containment of large volumes of goods. The main purpose of bulk packaging is to package goods at the lowest cost per delivery. The most popular materials for bulk packaging are bags, corrugated cardboard, metal, plastic, and wood. The factors affecting the decisions of bulk packaging materials include product weight and volume, costs, and product-related requirements such as temperature and loading compatibility.

5. *Transportation.* This dimension is concerned with the movement of finished products from warehouses to intermediaries or end users. Marketers must determine the modes of transportation to use. There are four major modes of transportation: railroads, roads, sea, and air. Which mode to use depends on a number of criteria: accessibility, reliability and safety, cost, and transit time. Table 9.1 compares the major modes of transportation based on these factors.

Summary

Distribution channels and logistics are two major elements of place—one of the marketing mix elements. The ultimate goal of channels and logistics planning is to ensure the right products get to the right customers, at the right price, at the right place, and at the right time. A marketing value chain provides a foundation for marketers to plan distribution channel and logistics issues in a holistic and proactive manner. Intermediaries within distributions channels perform transactional, physical, and facilitating functions in exchanges between manufacturers and end users. The decisions involved in designing distribution channels are the types of channel, the intensity of distribution, the specific intermediaries to use, and the motivational approaches to adopt. Logistics

Table 9.1. Comparison of Modes of Transportation

Modes of transportation			
Selection criteria	**Railroads**	**Roads**	**Sea**	**Air**
Accessibility	Low (rail tracks, dictating where a rail carrier goes)	High (provision of service to almost any location)	Low (only available to shippers adjacent to the waterway)	Low (requiring road carriers to transport freight to and from the airport)
Reliability and safety	High (weather conditions causing only minor problem)	Medium (weather conditions likely causing delay)	High	Low (weather affecting air service severely)
Cost	Low	High	Low	High
Transit time	Long	Medium (lower than railroads and sea, but higher than air)	Long	Short
Products most suitable	Long distance and bulky (e.g., timber)	Short distance and high-value (e.g., household goods)	Bulky, low-value, and nonperishable (e.g., toys)	High-value, perishable, or both (e.g., computer chips)

planning, which is concerned with the physical movements of products, involves six major tasks. They are order processing, warehousing, inventory management, materials handling, packaging and unitization, and transportation.

Chapter Review

1. Use an example of a real company to explain the driving forces of the marketing value chain management.
2. Design distribution channels for a brand new cosmetic product line. Justify your answers.
3. Establish a detailed logistics plan for a watch or clock manufacturer for its domestic market.

CHAPTER 10

Marketing Implementation and Control

Most of this book up to this point has been dedicated to showing how to analyze internal and external situations, how to set marketing objectives, and how to design marketing strategies. Marketing implementation and control are the last two steps in building a successful marketing plan. Marketing implementation and control should be based on the predetermined marketing objectives and strategies. Marketing implementation and control are practical actions to ensure that the set marketing strategies are carried out smoothly to reach the marketing objectives. Marketing strategies are no more than items on a wish list if they are not implemented properly. Up to 5% of marketing edge is created by marketing strategies and 95% by implementation.[1] Control plays a role as a gauge to provide feedback for marketers to identify any required corrective actions. Marketing implementation and control should be an integrated part of a marketing plan, rather than considered as backstage events that need limited attention.

Learning Objectives

After studying this chapter, you will be able to

- discuss the issues in relation to marketing implementation,
- explain a basic four-step control process,
- identify the tools for measuring marketing progress.

Marketing Implementation

Marketing implementation is defined as "the aspects of organizational structure and behavior that determine how a given strategy is carried out."[2] The ultimate goal of marketing implementation is to put marketing strategies into practice so that marketing objectives are achieved. The traditional view of an organization's ability to implement its strategy relies on the relationship between the organization's strategy and structure.[3] However, a contemporary view of implementation recognizes that other components, which are interrelated, also would affect the implementation of the organization's strategy. McKinsey consultants developed a comprehensive framework for effective strategy implementation, which consists of seven components—the McKinsey Seven S (7S) framework. The seven components of the framework—structure, strategy, systems, skills, staff, style, and superordinate goals (otherwise known as shared values).[4] All the elements other than *strategy* are related to implementation. *Strategy*, *structure*, and *systems* can be classified as the hardware elements. *Shared values*, *skills*, *staff*, and *style* are considered to be the software components.

Structure

Structure consists of the organization chart and related information that demonstrate who reports to whom and how tasks are allocated. The organization structure sets out authority and responsibility for the staff so that members can carry out the marketing strategies. When designing an appropriate structure, marketers have three major concerns: formalization, centralization, and specialization.

> Within an organizational structure, "formalization is the degree to which formal rules and standard policies and procedures govern decisions and working relationships, while centralization refers to the location of decision authority and control within an organization's hierarchy, and specialization refers to the division of tasks and activities across positions within the organizational unit."[5]

The combination of a high level of formalization and centralization with a low level of specialization is likely to perform comparatively efficiently. Formal rules and standard policies provide clear and specific guidelines that, in turn, reduce risk and administrative costs. However, the downside is that such a structure is slow to adapt to ever-changing external environments and restricts innovation. A high level of formalized structure can have a negative impact on implementing a marketing orientation.[6] On the other hand, decentralization, with a lower level of formalization and more specialists present, is likely to be more flexible and encourage innovation.

Basically, there are four types of organizational structures. They are functional, product or brand specialization, geographic specialization, and matrix. Figures 10.1–10.4 show all four types of organizational structures.

The functional structure is the simplest structure, and it is popular among smaller organizations. With this structure, a manager is responsible for each functional area. It well suits organizations with a small product range, few markets to serve, major decisions being made by high-ranking staff, and specialization required by function.

When organizations expand, functional managers may find it hard to keep up with the pace of functional activities across a range of different products or brands. One of the ways to deal with this situation is to adopt a product or brand management organization structure. This structure decentralizes decision making and increases the level of product specialization. It works well when products are complex and technical; are unrelated or dissimilar, such as furniture, toys, and watches; and consist of a large number of individual items. A good example is the thousands of hardware items offered by a wholesaler.

Figure 10.1. Functional structure incorporating the marketing concept.

Figure 10.2. Product/brand specialization structure incorporating the marketing concept.

The geographic specialization structure is similar to the product or brand specialization structure in that decision making is decentralized. It is, likewise, suitable for organizations with a broader product range. However, geographic specialization structures, as the name suggests, center marketing and selling activities in specific geographic areas. Each marketing or sales manager is responsible for his or her assigned region. It works well when special knowledge about geographic regions is important and fast responses to the marketing needs of varying geographic regions are critical.

The matrix structure is the least centralized and the most specialized among the four types of organization structures. With this structure, each

Figure 10.3. Geographic specialization structure incorporating the marketing concept.

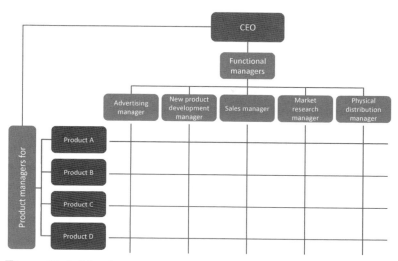

Figure 10.4. Matrix management structure.

staff member may have two or more reporting links. For example, a sales-person may need to report to both a sales manager and a brand manager. It is appropriate when the organization is in an extremely complex and uncertain business environment and when high levels of flexibility are needed to handle intrinsically dynamic markets.

Systems

Systems refer to the established procedures by which organizations con-duct daily operational activities and monitor the outcomes of procedures. Some important systems include accounting and budgeting systems, marketing information systems, and measurement and reward systems.

1. *Accounting and budgeting systems.* These are important systems that contain valuable historical quantitative data used to inform market-ers of exactly how productive or nonproductive marketing programs perform in terms of revenues, costs, profits, and returns. An exam-ple of this system is the chart of weekly sales numbers by product line.

2. *Marketing information systems.* These include technology, data-bases, models, and expert systems that provide a continuous flow

of information for marketers to understand the activities of their markets and marketing activities. For example, the link between the marketing information systems of a marketer and a retailer provides the necessary information for the retailer to replenish inventories and for the marketer to handle new orders.

3. *Measurement and reward systems.* The measurement and reward systems can drive employee behaviors, affecting strategy implementation. It is important to have a system that links rewards to measures of performance. Monetary rewards are believed to be an important tool to motivate staff, but other forms of rewards, such as praise, recognition, titles, reserved parking spaces, and bigger offices, can also be powerful motivators. One imperative issue when designing the measurement and reward system is to ensure the measures of performance reflect a long-term perspective in order to balance short-term results.[7]

These systems may be simple or multifaceted, manual or automated, generating qualitative or quantitative information, or producing reports on a weekly, monthly, or annual basis. In every instance, the systems should be in place to facilitate marketing implementation.

Shared Values

Shared values represent commonly held beliefs, mindsets, and assumptions that specify what is important to an organization's management and that guide how an organization acts. The shared values align all actions and keep the staff working toward common objectives as a functioning group. Shared values are the glue in organizations.[8] Without the glue to hold the organization together, organization staff members may focus their actions in different areas. Clear and strong values are widely accepted in the organization, and in effect staff members are able to identify them and understand their underlying principles. The organizations with weak shared values often find their staff pursuing their own personal goals that may be different or even in conflict with those of the organization,[9] consequently adversely affecting the success of the organization as a whole. Two recommended methods of creating shared values are employee training and socialization programs.[10] Creating or shifting shared values is not an easy task. It is a long-term process. Marketers (through comprehensive internal marketing programs) need to be patient and persevere when trying to create shared values.

Skills

Skills are related to an organization's distinctive capabilities and competencies. The distinctive capabilities and competencies indicate what the organization does best. Staff members need competent skills to implement marketing strategies. Marketing staff must be able to work with staff from other departments, such as production, engineering, and procurement. They need to have good communication skills to get the messages across and interpersonal skills to work with others to get the marketing strategies implemented. Marketing staff also need to acquire skills to deal with issues raised by external factors, such as customers' and distributors' needs and complaints.

Training and orientation programs are crucial in developing skills for marketing staff. Orientation provides marketing staff members with the necessary information they need to know to perform their jobs and the expectations they are supposed to reach. These programs indicate what skills they should possess and at what levels their skills need to be. In addition to formal training, programs that facilitate marketing staff to improve their skills and information sharing as to how to do business in an informal manner among marketing staff can assist in building staff competencies.

Staff

Organizations are made up of humans, and the staff can make the real difference to the success of any implementation of marketing strategies. In today's increasingly knowledge-based society, staff becomes a critical asset to organizations. Through staff selection, training, motivation, and evaluation, organizations can attract and retain the suitable and competent staff who are needed to implement marketing strategies and achieve the organization's objectives.

Selection

The first step in managing staff is employee recruitment and selection. Organizations first need to understand what exactly they expect from potential employees and how their jobs are carried out. Differing employees tend to excel at different tasks (e.g., dealing with people, public speaking, or being detail oriented). Thus a critical issue in implementation is to match employees' skills and abilities to the marketing tasks they need to perform.

Training

Training has been briefly discussed in the previous skills section. The major purpose of training is to ensure that employees are equipped with the necessary capabilities to perform their tasks and ultimately attain the organization's objectives. One point worthy of noting is that each employee is different to a certain extent. Training practices, especially informal training such as mentoring, may need to be adapted to suit individual employees.

Motivation

There are a number of ways to motivate employees. Financial compensation is an obvious factor to motivate staff to implement marketing strategies successfully. Other than financial compensation, some nonfinancial compensation, such as helping staff achieving their self-fulfillment goals or their involvement in the development of goals for the organization, can also serve to motivate staff members in their push for excellence.

Evaluation

Staff performance in terms of implementing marketing strategies needs to be evaluated continuously. Outcome-based systems and behavior-based systems are two options for organizations to evaluate staff performance.[11] Outcome-based systems are the use of measureable, quantitative standards, such as sales volume and profit margin, while behavior-based systems adopt subjective, qualitative standards, such as exertion, team collaboration, and even friendliness, to evaluate the successfulness of market implementation. The former systems are easier to measure, require less administration, and encounter less office politics. The latter systems tie evaluation directly to customer satisfaction levels and evaluate staff members for factors within their control.

Style

The styles of organizations conducting business are a key component of their corporate culture. A corporate culture consists of the dominant values, attitudes, beliefs, norms, and ways of doing business that become relatively permanent features of organizations. The role of style is completely different to that of systems and structure. The latter, as discussed in the previous sections, depend on explicit and structured manners to implement marketing strategies. The former relies on informal rules, such as norms of behavior and attitudes toward an action, that affect decisions and actions throughout an organization by indicating what constitutes acceptable attitudes and behavior. There are no definitively right or wrong, or good or bad, styles. A style that works for one organization may not work well for another. Cultivating a desired style entails regular communication from senior managers so that expected progress and actions about marketing strategies can be developed. A desired style can be developed and maintained by symbolic action. Some commonly used symbols of this action are activities, asking questions, and role models.

Activities

The activities that senior marketers are involved in and focused upon can have a significant impact on an organization's style. To lead by example is one of the ways a senior marketer creates a desired style—for instance, a marketing executive getting heavily involved in a new product development process signifies the importance of the introduction of new products to the organization.

Questions

A senior marketer can focus on an issue or shift a focus to another issue by continually and intentionally asking questions about the issue(s) that she or he would like to stress. In the new product development example noted in the prior paragraph, a senior marketer can ask questions in formal or informal meetings about competitors' new product situations and the status of the organization's new product development. Once the same types of questions are asked several times, the issue is more likely to become a focal point for the organization.

Role Models

Role models employed within organizations communicate and demonstrate different styles to show what values and beliefs each organization holds. Steve Jobs of Apple concentrating on product innovation and Lou Gersner of IBM shifting the focus to marketing create a clear expression of their values and provide a direction for the staff to follow in implementing each organization's strategies.

The Basic Control Process

Control is a process whereby marketers monitor the performance of marketing strategies on an ongoing basis to ensure that the predetermined objectives are achieved. It is defined as "a set of organized actions directed toward achieving specified goals in the face of constraints."[12]

Control allows marketers to understand where organizations stand in terms of performance. The whole control process requires that marketing performance can be observed, measured, and redirected if actions need to be taken to remedy discrepancies between the objectives and the actual performance. The specific, measurable, achievable, realistic, and time-bound (SMART) approach in setting objectives is a useful framework for setting performance standards. Control should be considered as part of the planning process because it complements the planning process. The planning process is not complete without considering controlling issues.

There are three major characteristics for an effective control process:

1. It should be flexible enough to allow managers to respond as necessary to unexpected events.
2. It should provide accurate information, giving a true picture of managers' performance.
3. It should supply managers with the information in a timely manner because making decisions on the basis of outdated information is a recipe for failure.[13]

The first characteristic suggests that the marketers should be flexible in their plan. A plan is not set in stone. Because of the volatile nature of the external environment, it is important to have the flexibility to make changes in response to new situations. Resources should also be made available for necessary corrective actions.

The second characteristic concerning the accuracy of information to be provided to managers is related to the systems mentioned in the previous section. The systems should be able to provide relevant information for marketers so that they know where they are and where to go. In addition to the need for relevant information, the control process also should provide timely information. Timely information does not necessarily denote daily reports on every aspect of marketing. Instead, it simply means the timing for provision of information for the control process should reflect the nature of the marketing activities. For example, weekly information in regards to market share of a brand may not be necessary; reports every three to six months are more "timely" in this aspect.

There are four key steps in designing the control process as shown in Figure 10.5.

Setting Standards of Performance

Performance standards are mainly based on the set objectives and marketing strategies, as discussed in detail in chapter 4. With the performance standards in place, marketers have knowledge about what performance needs to be measured. Unclear or missing performance standards can adversely affect the other three steps in the control process. Based on the performance standards, organizations need to create measuring tools so that staff members know with what and how to measure performance.

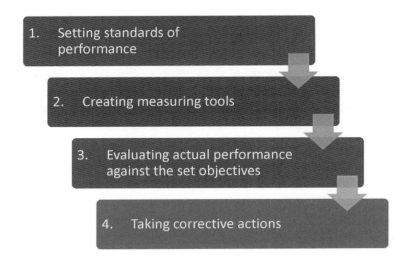

Figure 10.5. Designing the control process.

Measuring Marketing Progress: Tools

Once an organization has set performance standards, its next step in the control process is to create measuring tools for evaluating whether these standards are being achieved. In some cases, measuring performance is a very straightforward process. For instance, counting the number of new customers for a wholesaler is a simple tally. However, in some cases, measuring performance is a complicated endeavor, due to the fact that a marketing strategy may involve activities and staff across various departments. The root cause(s) for failure of a new product might be very difficult to pin down, as they might be found in one or more areas, such as research and development, advertising, distribution, or pricing. In view of this, tools used for measuring marketing progress must be as comprehensive as possible. The three main tools for measuring marketing progress are budgets, programming, and metrics.

Budgets

Budgets project revenues and expenses for a specific time period. They can be considered as blueprints that regulate how marketers intend to use the organization's resources to accomplish the organization's objectives.

They provide a benchmark for marketers to continuously compare actual performance against planned objectives. When actual performances deviate from the objectives, marketers may need to understand the underlying factors causing the deviation by breaking down the data to identify the problem. For example, a lower than expected return on investment requires marketers to break down the data for each product line and sales territory to determine exactly where the problem lies.

Sales and marketing cost analyses are the two major tools in budgetary control. Sales analysis is concerned with identifying the problem areas in relation to sales performance. The total sales figure of an organization indicates sales performance in general, but it does not present a complete picture of the organization's performance. An important issue in an organization's sales analysis is to decide what breakdowns to analyze. The most commonly adopted breakdowns are as follows:

- Product—by product line, product, and package size
- Geographical area—by regions, such as countries, states, and sales territories
- Customer—by type (e.g., different market segments)
- Type of channel/intermediary—by type (e.g., supermarkets, hypermarkets, discount stores, and drugstores)
- Size of order—by price points (e.g., under $10, $11–15, $16–20, and so on)
- Personal sales figures

Marketing cost analysis is a detailed study of the breakdowns of marketing costs in relation to specific marketing activities. Similar to the sales analysis, an overall figure, marketing cost in this case indicates very little about the profitability of marketing activities. Marketing cost should be broken down into a number of categories to gain further insights as stated in sales analysis. The comparison of the actual costs and estimated costs of each breakdown is likely to offer more useful information. Marketing cost analysis is more complicated than sales analysis. First, more items need to be evaluated (e.g., logistics and marketing administrative costs). Second, appropriate cost allocation can be quite problematic. Marketing costs can be divided into direct and indirect costs. Direct costs are those incurred completely in relation to one particular category.

Therefore, the promotional expenses for territory Z are direct costs for that territory. The logistics and order processing costs for a product line are direct costs for that specific product line. Allocating direct costs is straightforward. The allocation problem lies in the indirect costs, which are incurred mutually for more than one marketing category. The salary of the marketing director and the rent of an office are two examples of indirect costs. Determining how much of these costs to allocate to each category is debatable and usually negotiable.

Programming

Programming is sometimes called scheduling. It involves identification, coordination, and completion of particular action programs within specified timelines. Some examples are a new product launch or an advertising campaign for a repositioned brand. Programming is a nonfinancial control tool. Programs should be developed on the basis of the organization's objectives and marketing strategies. Programming usually requires substantial details. All programs related to marketing activities should be incorporated in the plan, and each program should show starting and ending dates, staff responsibilities for the activities, and the main tasks of each program. In other words, programming addresses the issues of who does what and by when. The detailed programs about the various marketing activities provide marketers with a platform to monitor progress and to evaluate the results of a program to determine if the objectives are being achieved.

Metrics

Another tool available for marketers to measure marketing process is metrics. Metrics are "specific, numerical standards used on a regular basis to measure selected performance-related activities and outcomes."[14] Metrics are vital to organizations because they are precise, consistent, and comprehensive.[15] At a macro level, they represent a complete control process. At the micro level, metrics can indicate what measure to use to determine if the organization's marketing strategies are effective and efficient. The major concerns of this tool are what to measure in determining the performances of marketing activities and how to go about measuring it. The specific metrics to use depend on the organization's mission, objectives, and marketing strategies. Metrics can be used to measure profitability and profit margins, sales levels, product awareness, and number of new products, among others.[16] Metrics can also be used to measure areas of marketing planning and customers, the offering (the marketing mix), and sales force.[17] Expanding the scope further, metrics can measure the share of hearts, minds, and markets; finance; operations, logistics; the trade; and advertising media and the web.[18]

When choosing metrics, marketers need to consider a number of issues. First, the selected metrics should be instrumental in the success of the organization. Second, quantified metrics should measure both financial and nonfinancial performances. Finally, metrics should evaluate performance in a manner that allows further actions to be taken, if necessary.

Evaluating Actual Performance Against the Set Objectives

The third step in the control process is to evaluate the actual performance against the predetermined objectives. Marketers can evaluate the actual performance using a variety of information generated from various systems and market research. Organizations can utilize this step as a signal system to diagnose deviations. Three potential performance outcomes can be expected from this step. They can be either higher than the objectives, in line with the objectives, or lower than the objectives. When performance is higher or lower than the objectives, marketers need to discover the reasons for such deviations. Some reasons may be beyond the control of the marketers, such as a financial crisis or a terrorist attack that had a negative impact on the general marketplace economy. In other situations, marketers may be able to act quickly to respond to factors that affect the organization's performance; the low awareness of an introduction of a new brand is one example of this. In either case, the final step in the control process is needed. Marketers must take necessary actions to remedy the adverse situations.

Taking Corrective Actions

Corrective actions may be in the form of adjusting the objectives or changing marketing strategies. The remedial actions to be taken depend on the situation and the organization's objectives. The success of corrective action relies on the third step, the evaluating step. At times, this may entail gathering further information before making a decision about what action to take. Marketers, in some situations, may need to take action quickly, while in others, they may have more time to evaluate broader options. Corrective actions trigger another cycle of marketing strategy formulation, implementation, and control.

Summary

Marketing implementation and control are inseparable parts of a marketing plan. The main purpose of marketing implementation is to carry out marketing strategies so as to reach marketing objectives. The McKinsey 7S model—which consists of strategy, structure, systems, shared values, skills, staff, and style—is an effective tool for ensuring all the bases are covered during marketing implementation. While marketing implementation is concerned with the actions to execute marketing strategies, the main purpose of control is to monitor the performance and to detect any deviations from the predetermined marketing objectives. The four key steps in the control process are setting standards of performance, creating measuring tools, evaluating actual performance against the predetermined objectives, and taking corrective actions. The control process ends a marketing planning cycle and triggers another.

Chapter Review

1. Assume that you are a senior marketing staff of an airline company; devise an implementation plan for a marketing campaign of a new international route.
2. Describe the basic four-step control process. Use the example of the airline in question 1 to illustrate the basic control process.

Pindari Boomerang Factory Marketing Plan Example

Marketing Plan

Our mission:

To create a better quality of life and standing in the community for indigenous people through the promotion of indigenous culture and employment opportunities.

—Pindari (meaning "from the high ground" or "high rocks")

Executive Summary

Pindari Boomerang Factory is located in Central Queensland near the city of Rockhampton. Pindari Boomerang Factory (Pindari) was officially incorporated on June 10, 2000. Recommendations for Pindari based on the analysis in this marketing plan for the next 12 months to 2 years of operation are summarized by the following strategies:

Strategy 1: Product Strategy

Pindari must work to develop sample ranges of products for each of the major target markets—therefore two separate ranges based on the product lines as described in item 2.4. The company must develop a further sample product range to cater to the niche market requirements of local tourism industry enterprises (also described at item 2.4).

Strategy 2: Product Strategy

Pindari must design and develop packaging for the duty-free market. The company should establish contacts with The Box Company to develop individualized packaging for prestige Pindari product lines.

Strategy 3: Product Strategy

Pindari must design and develop packaging (such as canvas carry bags with artwork) for didgeridoos. Packaging can be developed within the community using screen printing techniques for transferring designs onto canvas or calico materials. If suitable designs can be developed, material can also be used as tablecloths and napkins in local restaurants for display and distributed to industry outlets for sale.

Strategy 4: Pricing Strategy

Pindari should utilize a competitor-based pricing strategy for the duty-free target market range and for the drive-through target market range. The competitor-based strategy examines competitor pricing for equivalent or substitute items and sets Pindari's prices for such items at equal or slightly lower values than currently established in the market. This will provide Pindari with a slight competitive advantage and enable easier market entry.

During the establishment of the sample ranges, careful analysis should be made of the costs for manufacture of each item or line so that detailed cost structures can be entered into the financial information spreadsheet. It is imperative that Pindari understand the financial and time costs of manufacture of individual product items if production on a larger scale is to be feasible.

Note: Calculations for the profit and loss statement have been performed based on prices set using this method.

Strategy 5: Distribution Strategy

To access the local, drive-through market, Pindari should have distribution on a much smaller and more manageable scale. Within 12 months of start-up, Pindari needs to establish a minimum of five new contacts for distribution of product within the Central Queensland region to capture the drive-through market on the heritage trails routes.

Strategy 6: Promotion Strategy

Pindari should promote tourism growth in Rockhampton city and sales growth by partnering with a selection of other tourism operators. Pindari must secure a working agreement with two tourism operators within the following 12 months to enable cooperation between the parties to market Pindari as a destination (at least for day-trips from Rockhampton). Primary players in the city area should work together to build a day-trip package tour. This strategy aims to provide Pindari with a minimum of through traffic. This is a long-term strategy and will require careful planning but should aim to be running within 2 years of start-up.

Strategy 7: Promotion Strategy

Pindari should develop a brochure to be placed in tourist information centers throughout Central Queensland. The brochure should be no more than a threefold A4 sheet that presents the story of Pindari and the indigenous community, as well as promoting Pindari products. A combined brochure for the day-trip tour is also an option and will require further investigation.

Strategy 8: Branding Strategy

Pindari should develop history cards to be included with products. Pindari needs to differentiate its product from others developed and sold by different indigenous communities throughout Australia. Pindari should develop story cards for each of the products in the range. Other cards can be developed depicting the artists and their stories to be sold with special artwork, such as canvases.

Further, the company should develop a story card that provides insight into Pindari itself as the product's branding. Branding is particularly important for the international market, as international visitors require authenticity and an understanding of the product's origins, the company's origins, and the origins of the people who created these artworks or artifacts. The company should develop profiles (including personal information or history and photographic images) of the indigenous artists to be included with products and on story boards to be posted around Pindari's main operation center.

Strategy 9: Branding Strategy

Pindari must establish contact with the various indigenous and Torres Strait Islander agencies, including Indigenous Tourism Australia and the Indigenous Tourism Leadership Group to gain membership to training programs and also to gain authenticity badging for Pindari products. It is particularly important to be regarded as authentic product producers to gain sales and brand equity in the international tourism market. The branding strategy aims to be an umbrella brand (one identity for all products in the range).

Contents

Illustrations

Figures

Tables

Pindari Boomerang Factory Marketing Plan

1 Our Mission

"To create a better quality of life and standing in the community for indigenous people through the promotion of indigenous culture and employment opportunities."

2 The Business

2.1 Description and Brief History of the Business

Pindari Boomerang Factory (Pindari) is based in Central Queensland, about a 40-minute drive from the city of Rockhampton. Pindari was officially incorporated on June 10, 2000, by the board of directors, including the owner and CEO and a partner who is the enterprise art director. Starting with just the two principle staff members, the corporation aimed to produce indigenous art and artifacts (including painted artifacts, such as didgeridoos, boomerangs, pottery, canvases, emu eggs, and other authentic products). These works were initially for sale locally with eventual growth to statewide and interstate markets. The long-term view is to eventually export overseas. Pindari Boomerang Factory is a not-for-profit, incorporated body. As such, the business is under direct indigenous control with profit sharing among members and the possibility of shared control of the enterprise.

The factory initially operated on land leased from the Queensland state government. When the lease reverted to the state, the operation had to be moved. Once the factory found a suitable venue to relocate, Pindari was reestablished at its current site. In 2003 Pindari Boomerang Factory purchased the land, and in 2004 the company built a three-bay shed with the aid of government funding. The enterprise has continued to grow (if slowly) at this location over the past 6 years.

2.2 Business Structure

The business is run by the CEO and board of directors, as demonstrated in the flow chart in appendix A. The business has been operating with just six general staff members (five in manufacturing and one part-time administration assistant), as well as the CEO and the art director. Of the three full-time manufacturing staff members, two cut templates, while the third paints on a rotational basis. A casual staff member works on larger orders, and the company has a trainee. The part-time office administration assistant provides general enterprise bookkeeping, order taking, and other administrative duties as required and is overseen by the partner (who is also the art director).

Further, Pindari has an extensive network of indigenous community members who also provide various artworks and artifacts into the enterprise (though mostly on an ad hoc basis).

2.3 Goals

The long-term goals of the enterprise are as follows:

- Create employment for indigenous people in Central Queensland.
- Foster pride in indigenous culture among indigenous people.
- Encourage independence and self-determination for indigenous people.
- Become a self-funded organization that is not reliant on continued government funding.
- Increase understanding of indigenous culture within the non-indigenous community.
- Promote tourism and foster a positive image in Central Queensland.

2.4 Products

The products are broken up into three product lines based around the two market segments—**drive-through market** products and **duty-free market** products—in line with Pindari's target markets.

2.4.1 BOOMERANGS: DRIVE-THROUGH MARKET PRODUCTS

- Nonflying boomerangs produced in three sizes, including the following:
  - Small—6 or 10 inches
  - Medium—16 inches
  - Large—18 inches
- Construction from hardwood timber sheets 3,000 mm long by 1,700 mm wide by 12-mm thick cuts down to 10 mm thick on a finished boomerang. Using a template, three boomerangs can be cut from a single section.
- The boomerangs are all decorative. Because they are manufactured from hardwood, the pieces will not fly. Adding a small range of flying boomerangs will also be attractive to this market due to the customers' greater "hands-on" approach to travel and the travel experience.
- Timber is available from two local hardwood suppliers.
- Designs include traditional indigenous depictions such as the kangaroo, crocodile, platypus, emu, snake, porcupine, and turtle.
- Production costs include the following:
  - *Labor time for cutting and shaping boomerangs.* Using the band saw, it takes approximately 10 minutes to cut the initial shapes, approximately 20 seconds to shape a boomerang with the router, 2 minutes per boomerang to finish the shape with a sander, and then about 1 minute to finish on the drum sander.
  - *Painting time per boomerang.* It takes 20 to 25 seconds for three people to paint the colors, including one painting the outlines and the ends, one painting the stroke line colors, and one painting the dot colors. Finally, one person will oil the boomerangs.

2.4.2 BOOMERANGS: DUTY-FREE MARKET PRODUCTS

Specialist designs are sold to the prestige tourist market in a selection of Sydney (Darling Harbor) duty-free stores, Sydney International Airport duty-free stores, Brisbane Queen Street Mall, and Brisbane International Airport duty-free stores.

These specialty boomerangs ostensibly remain the same product with added packaging and a display stand. Packaging is supplied by The Box Company at 1,000 boxes per order, though at present these packages are not branded with a Pindari logo or labeling. Pindari should provide short cultural stories or narratives with each product to value add a cultural experience to the product. Pindari could gain authenticity recognition by including the authentic indigenous art or craft logo on product packaging. Again, these products are nonflying due to their hardwood construction.

2.4.3 OTHER PRODUCTS

The following products are designed for both the drive-through and duty-free markets, although, as before, the duty-free market display and packaging will need to be investigated further.

DIDGERIDOOS

The didgeridoo market is a growth area for indigenous culture and artifacts. Didgeridoo construction requires blanks to be purchased from local timber mills and generally takes approximately 1 to 2 hours to construct, which includes painting. The designs are the same as on the boomerangs, including traditional indigenous depictions such as the kangaroo, crocodile, platypus, emu, snake, porcupine, and turtle.

In the didgeridoo market, it is vitally important that Pindari separate itself and its products from those of other boomerang manufacturers through packaging and through the cultural stories. Pindari should manufacture a carry bag specifically for the didgeridoos with company depictions on it. The carry bag for the didgeridoos is important to act as protection in luggage holds and also as a further brand identity symbol for Pindari.

Bullroarers, Key Rings, Fridge Magnets, and Jewelry

Off-cut pieces and spare blanks are used to manufacture small, specialty products, including key rings, bullroarers, and fridge magnets. Also included are wooden jewelry pieces, such as earrings, necklaces, and bracelets. These pieces fall under the product classification of ancillary products and are becoming very popular for international and domestic markets.

3 Marketing Plan

3.1 External Environment

This section of the plan provides a brief overview of trends as they arise in the macroenvironment—that is, the various factors that the company has little control over.

3.1.1 Political Environment

The global political environment needs to be closely monitored given the current state of military unrest and political upheaval with the war in Iraq and the continuing issues of terrorism. While the Central Queensland community is largely separated from the major impacts of these issues, the international tourism visitation rates demonstrate the impacts on the tourism industry, which will affect tourist traffic available to Pindari.

The second issue specifically relevant to Pindari is the suggested federal government aim to limit unauthentic imports of indigenous products. This is a recent development and will also need to be monitored closely. The final area of concern is the federal government budget, which is due for release in May to June each year. This could have unexpected repercussions for indigenous corporations and tourism industry expenditure and must be continuously monitored.

3.1.2 Legal and Regulatory Environments

The legal or regulatory environment is stable at this time with regard to indigenous, nonprofit, corporation operation.

While individual art products (such as canvases) are still largely outside of the Pindari product range, the general market for souvenirs and representative samples of indigenous cultural products is large and growing. The industry for cultural artifacts is problematic however, with the development of inexpensive, unauthentic imported products (e.g., didgeridoos and boomerangs made in Taiwan and T-shirts designed and printed by nonindigenous producers).[1]

With regard to intellectual property rights,

> Cultural and Intellectual Property Rights for Indigenous Australians have been significant issues for the past three decades. Unfortunately, the protection of such rights has not been given the same priority as other pressing issues like health and native title. As indigenous culture attracts increasing commercial interest, indigenous people are concerned that they do not have the necessary rights to ensure appropriate recognition, protection and financial compensation for their contributions.[2]

There is a pressing need for an independent, economic evaluation of the facts by suitably qualified people and research into the impact of commercialization on indigenous cultures in Australia.

3.1.3 TECHNOLOGICAL ENVIRONMENT

The technological environment will affect Pindari directly because of the increased access to, and usage of, the Internet as an information and sales source for indigenous products. An initiative being promoted by AUSTRADE is an Internet facility that individual enterprises can use to market their products nationally and internationally. This can also double as a database of indigenous artists, to assist in spreading awareness of who is doing what in the industry and to encourage networking.[3]

Look into the Internet as an alternative form of distribution. Pindari can work in conjunction with the other indigenous and nonindigenous tourism industry operators to include a Pindari page on their site (to be negotiated) with a long-term view to developing a Pindari website.

3.1.4 SOCIOCULTURAL ENVIRONMENT

Increasingly, interest and growth in sales in the areas of indigenous culture, experience, and arts and handcrafts has been demonstrated from both international and domestic markets. There is increasing interest in cultural significance and regional difference as portrayed in indigenous art and performance.

> With this developing interest has come a finer appreciation among art lovers of the diversity of indigenous art, relating to regional differences in style and inspiration, and individual artistic expression. Several indigenous artists (both individuals and community-based enterprises) have achieved a considerable national and international reputation, with a consequent keen market for their products.[4]

Several types of markets for indigenous arts have been identified, with the main categories being as follows:

- *Functional fine art.* These products are made for secular or religious use rather than for purely commercial purposes, and they are firmly based in customary patterns of expression. They are bought by people with an interest in tradition and culture.
- *Commercial fine arts.* These products are made with eventual sale in mind but with a strong element of original artistic creativity based on cultural themes. The prime market is people who have a keen interest in artistic expression.
- *Tourist art.* These products are items that can be produced in a convenient size, weight, price, and adequate quantity to appeal to tourists as souvenirs, and they are produced for that purpose.[5]

By all accounts the appeal and status of Australian indigenous art and craft products and cultural experiences are increasing with sales demonstrating the growth of this industry. The Aboriginal and Torres Strait Islander Commission[6] estimated that the art and craft industry is worth approximately $200 million annually.

3.2 Competition

The total indigenous art and craft market is made up of a combination of the following:[7]

- Indigenous-owned or -operated retail galleries
- Smaller galleries or exhibiting spaces that are connected to indigenous organizations
- Domestic retail sales, including mass-produced, nonindigenous products
- Handcrafted, authentic products
- Wholesale exports
- Sales to international visitors through duty-free stores and retail outlets owned/operated by nonindigenous operators

The manufacturing and sale of indigenous art and craft products is very diverse and often very competitive. As discussed in item 3.3.1, the industry is made up of several segments, including indigenous-owned or -operated retail galleries, smaller galleries, or exhibiting spaces that are connected to indigenous organizations; domestic retail sales including mass-produced, nonindigenous products and handcrafted, authentic products; wholesale exports; and sales to international visitors through duty-free stores and retail outlets owned or operated by nonindigenous operators.

The major competitors are broken up into geographic areas given Pindari's focus on Central Queensland trade as the primary target with the duty-free market as the secondary target market:

- Rockhampton and Central Queensland
- North and West Queensland
- Interstate

3.2.1 ROCKHAMPTON AND CENTRAL QUEENSLAND COMPETITORS[8]
Pindari's largest direct competitor in the local area is the Indigenous Culture Experience (ICE). ICE has an extensive range of products with added benefits of accommodation and tours.

ICE's strengths include its established history and its location, which has easy access and parking facilities for the drive-through market (Pindari's major target market). ICE also has ties with other local operators, which provide customers with package deals to the attractions. ICE has the added distinctive advantage of an online presence, which is well organized and has the option to purchase or gain further product information.

ICE's facilities and services include the following:

- An artifacts shop—a retail outlet to purchase authentic indigenous Australian artifacts and souvenirs
- Accommodation for up to 15 guests
- Two conference facility areas

ICE's product range is shown in Table 1.

3.2.2 NORTH AND WEST QUEENSLAND COMPETITORS

Two other major direct competitors in Queensland are the Indigenous Cultural Park (ICP) and Aboriginal Arts and Crafts (AAC). These two operators have been particularly singled out for their Internet presence and the capacity to purchase a range of products that match those offered by Pindari. A number of other indigenous and Torres Strait Islander operations throughout the state also are direct competitors and will need to be considered in the long term.

Table 1. Indigenous Culture Experience Product and Price List

Item	Price ($)
Donna Hansen bush game	22.00
Large boomerang (right hand and left hand)	16.50
Three-pronged boomerangs	17.00
Clap sticks	29.95
Branded teaspoons (gold and silver)	5.45
Branded letter opener	5.85
Branded hatpin	3.75
Branded fridge magnet	2.60
Branded key rings	6.95
Didgeridoo music CD	24.20
Aboriginal design T-shirts (two colors)	44.85
Aboriginal design T-shirts (one color)	19.85
Traditional art boards	75.00
Traditional art canvas	95.00
Didgeridoo (bamboo)	55.00
Didgeridoo (hardwood)	160.00
Various books	Various

INDIGENOUS CULTURAL PARK

ICP is a large indigenous operation located in Far North Queensland. Initially a dance theatre, the attraction has grown to incorporate a 25-acre park, which is owned and operated by the local indigenous councils and peoples. Two of ICP's greatest strengths are its length of time in operation and its continued commitment to indigenous economic benefits.

ICP offers customers the following:

- Theatres
- Restaurants
- Night shows
- Day tours
- Packages

ICP's product range is extensive, with a large number of individual artistic suppliers contributing (see Table 2).

Table 2. Indigenous Cultural Park Product and Price List

Item	Price ($)
Didgeridoo—small bark on plain	280.00
Didgeridoo—large bark on plain	390.00
Didgeridoo—painted bloodwood (1st class)	470.00
Didgeridoo—Carved mallee (1st class)	890.00
Boomerang—(flying plywood, 18 inches)	15.00–39.00
Boomerang—Wangal cross returner (16 inches)	39.00
Boomerang—5 plywood, returning, no art	39.00
Boomerang—hardwood, no art	39.00
Boomerang—hardwood, painted (large range of sizes)	6.50–44.00
Ironwood clap sticks (flat style)	27.00
Acacia clap sticks (round style)	33.00
Hand-painted emu eggs	120.00
Aboriginal design T-shirts (large range)	24.95–34.00
Branded spray jackets	76.00
Various other art panels, prints, books, music, pottery	Various

ABORIGINAL ARTS AND CRAFTS (AAC)

Aboriginal Arts and Crafts (AAC) offers outsourcing for specific items and also the ability to export nationally and internationally. Prices are not included here as they are only available on application or order. AAC products are locally made by communities located in the Mount Isa region of North West Queensland (see Table 3).

3.2.3 INTERSTATE AND INTERNATIONAL COMPETITORS

The range of indigenous products (handicraft, artifacts, and tools) and performances is extensive. After a comprehensive search of the Internet, trade journals, and the Department of State Development, interstate and international competitors include retailers and wholesalers in both indigenous-owned and -operated facilities and nonindigenous operations. The majority of interstate operators are located in New South Wales and the Northern Territory, which indicates that the drive market (Pindari's major market) is very competitive with the border access points from both the west and south already reaching saturation.

Each of the following competitors is described briefly with its main strengths demonstrated. While each of the competitors offers unique products (unique to its location, culture, and identity), the competitors also have several factors in common that Pindari will need to match or in some way counter to gain some portion of the market share and

Table 3. Aboriginal Arts and Crafts Product List

Item
Indigenous arts and crafts from communities around Mount Isa
Handmade grass mats and weaving
Clothing and fabrics
Art supplies
Art framing
Indigenous artifacts
Didgeridoos and spears
Boomerangs and coolamons
Art exhibitions held in-house
Art workshops
External sourcing of other products as required

attain some measure of competitive advantage. Pindari, therefore, should develop some of these product and company features.

- At least one unique product or product feature such as the following:
    - Educational materials (e.g., cassettes of music and instruction for the didgeridoos)
    - Materials for schools to teach students indigenous culture
    - Photos of the artists, stories or information about them, or both
    - Local stories and stories about the artifacts or paintings
    - Family- or community-owned operations or artworks from a small number of communities
    - Some means of export (either by the Internet or by overseas representatives)
    - Stories about the community and its heritage and history
- A certificate of authenticity, authenticity labels, or both that are nationally accepted and accredited
- Specialization in one or two art areas, such as canvas paintings, didgeridoos, or framed works on bark
- Specialization in a particular technique such as burnings
- Professional presentation of the website
- Generally offer the capacity to purchase over the Internet using secure features
- Photo galleries of the product ranges

The following examples of some of the interstate competitors fall under two categories. Initially, some of the operations have product and price lists included in their analysis to offer examples of the product ranges. Then presented is a listing of a number of operations that have a summary of their business and their major strengths.

Outback Art

Outback Art is located in Melbourne, Victoria. The following product listing demonstrates its specialization in quality items and its aim to attract a more prestigious market segment. The products are all framed and presented as display items rather than working or flying artifacts. The product range is relatively small (see Table 4).

Oz Indigenous

Oz Indigenous provides a wide range of original indigenous art and artifacts. It has a display at the national trade show (the gift fair), which is held annually in Sydney during February. It offers both retail and wholesale services, and products can be bought direct from the trade fair, in stores, or online. Prices are only available on application or order, so they have not been included here.

Indigenous Dreaming

Indigenous Dreaming only offers one product line: Indigenous artwork on adult T-shirts and polo shirts or children's T-shirts. The simplicity of the product line is not to be understated, however, as the products are unique and authentic, and the artist has chosen a niche market in which to operate, which is particularly profitable.

The Rainbow Snake

The Rainbow Snake stocks a range of products from indigenous artists across Australia. The company supports the National Indigenous Arts Advocacy Association's (NIAAA) label schemes by carrying goods that bear the label of authenticity or the collaboration mark and is working toward providing the majority of its indigenous products with the label of authenticity or the collaboration mark. It's located in the Sydney International Airport.

Table 4. Outback Art Product and Price List

Item	Price ($)
Framed painted boomerangs	
• Tiny hunter (dots or crosshatch)	99.00
• Small hunter (dots or crosshatch)	165.00
• Large hunter (dots or crosshatch)	387.00
Major paintings—range of sizes and prices	950.00–1650.00
Small paintings—range of sizes and prices	110.00–185.00
Didgeridoo—hand-burnt (140 cm)	350.00
Didgeridoo—hand-painted (130 cm)	190.00

INDIGENOUS EXPORTS

Indigenous Exports deals in fine art on quality linen or canvas (imported from Belgium) and is a distributor of indigenous arts, crafts, ceramics, didgeridoos, and boomerangs. The canvases are exported for both sale and display in museum and art galleries. The paintings are from indigenous communities located throughout South Australia, the Northern Territory, and Western Australia and are authenticated through authenticity certificates and photos of the artists. All paintings are also copyrighted to Indigenous Exports and the respective artists. It is located in Adelaide, South Australia.

INDIGENOUS AUSTRALIA

Indigenous Australia allows artifact shoppers to buy indigenous art and cultural items direct from an indigenous community enterprise trust–owned art gallery. The gallery is located in the Northern Territory of Australia. Indigenous Australia retails through the online medium with sales in art and cultural artifacts, while the center itself also offers indigenous tours and dance performances. The center exports to some 76 countries with a product range that includes art, didgeridoos, boomerangs, music, educational materials for schools, and clothing.

INDIGENOUS UK

Indigenous UK provides a range of top-quality eucalyptus didgeridoos specifically for musicians. The company also provides starter packs for learners of the instrument, including an economical "starter didg" and a cassette for instruction. Indigenous UK's product range also includes art, crafts, and musical instruments from around the world, T-shirts, hand-painted shirts, limited edition prints, fabric prints, carvings, clap sticks, bullroarers, and hand-crafted boomerangs. It is located at the Cotswolds in Worcestershire, England.

3.3 Customers: The Target Markets

The total market for Pindari products includes international, intrastate, and interstate visitors to, and within, Australia. Initially, Pindari will focus its efforts on two main market segments that have been chosen as those most serviceable for this small business due to their clearly identifiable qualities of measurability, substantiality, actionability, and accessibility.[9] Those target markets are defined as the following:

- Retail sales of handcrafted, authentic products through an indigenous-owned or -operated retail storefront (being Pindari's own manufacturing venue) and through other retail venues as may be considered suitable within the Capricorn tourism region (to be known as the drive market)
- Sales to international visitors through duty-free stores and retail outlets owned or operated by nonindigenous operators (initially within Sydney's Darling Harbor and Brisbane's Queen Street Mall stores as test markets and to be known as the duty-free market)

3.3.1 THE DRIVE MARKET

In 1999, the Capricorn region attracted 1.07 million visitors with the majority (nearly three quarters of the population) being intrastate visitors (those from within Queensland).[10] Figure 1 shows the visitor breakdown.

INTRASTATE VISITORS

In 2001, intrastate visitors still constituted the majority of visitors to Capricorn, and of those nearly three quarters were from regional Queensland

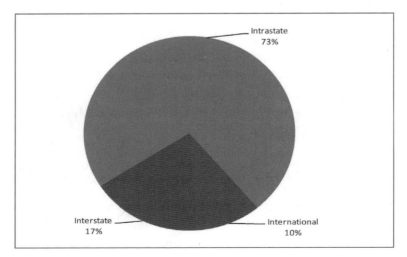

Figure 1. Capricorn markets visitor breakdown.

(only 27% of visitors were from Brisbane). The purpose of travel for intrastate visitors included vacation (39%), visiting friends and relatives (24%), and business (26%).[11]

INTERSTATE VISITORS

Some 78% of interstate visitors were from New South Wales (NSW) and Victoria with 29% of those from Sydney and 25% from Melbourne. Visitors from NSW recorded the longest lengths of stay, spending some 7.4 nights (on average) in the region. The purpose of travel for interstate visitors included vacation and visiting friends and relatives (39% each) and business (23%).[12]

INTERNATIONAL VISITORS

The international visitor market to the Capricorn region is much smaller than the domestic market. In 1999, just over 103,000 international visitors came to the region.[13] The purpose of travel for the majority of those visitors was vacation (81%). The major countries or regions of origin for the Capricorn region are shown in Figure 2.

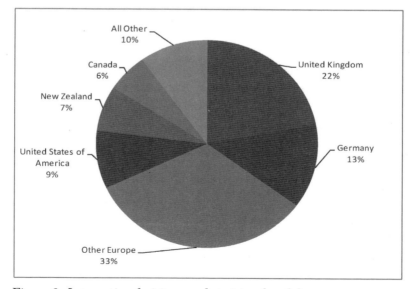

Figure 2. International visitor market visitor breakdown.

MODE OF TRANSPORT

The Capricorn region is heavily reliant on road travelers with some 84% of all domestic travelers to the region using a private vehicle. The largest portion of international visitors (38% of those who stop in Capricorn) also use private transport—a combination of rental car, self-drive van, motor home, or camper.[14]

3.3.2 DRIVE MARKET DEMOGRAPHICS AND TRAVEL BEHAVIOR

Tourism Queensland has defined the drive market as those persons "travelling away from home for at least one night, on holidays or visiting friends and relatives, in their own, a rented or borrowed, vehicle as the primary mode of transport."[15]

DOMESTIC DRIVE MARKET

The Queensland domestic drive market is broken up into four main market segments:[16]

- Short break visitors (staying one to two nights, of which 91% are Queensland intrastate visitors)
- Short tour visitors (staying four to seven nights, of which 70% are intrastate and 22% are from NSW)
- Big tour visitors (staying eight to 21 nights, of which 49% are from Queensland, 27% are from New South Wales, and 14% are from Victoria)
- Grand tour visitors (staying 22 nights or longer, of which 32% are from New South Wales, 29% are from Queensland, 26% are from Victoria, and 14% are from other states and territories)

INTERNATIONAL DRIVE MARKET

The international drive market (which is perhaps more important for Pindari given the information that nearly 50% of total sales of indigenous art and artifacts are to international visitors) has been defined as

any international visitor to Australia for the purpose of a holiday or visiting friends and relatives, who indicated that their main form of transport used between stopovers in Australia was a private or

Table 5. Top Three Characteristics of the Queensland Domestic Drive Market Segments[17]

Drive market segment	Travel party (visitors)	Life cycle (visitors)	Accommodation (visitor nights)	Activity (visitors)
Short break (1–3 nights)	1. Adult couple (32%) 2. Family group, parents & children (25%) 3. Traveling alone (19%)	1. Young/midlife couple, no kids (16%) 2. Parent with youngest child aged 6–14 (13%) 3. Parent with youngest child aged 5 or less (12%)	1. Friends' or relatives' property (47%) 2. Hotel, resort, motel, or motor inn (25%) 3. Rented house, apartment, unit, or flat (9%)	1. Visit friends and relatives (48%) 2. Eat out/restaurants (42%) 3. Go to the beach (including swimming, surfing, diving) (30%)
Short tour (4–7 nights)	1. Family group: parents & children (35%) 2. Adult couple (30%) 3. Traveling alone (16%)	1. Older nonworking married person (18%) 2. Parent with youngest child aged 6–14 (16%) 3. Parent with youngest child aged 5 or less (14%)	1. Friends' or relatives' property (37%) 2. Rented house, apartment, unit, or flat (23%) 3. Hotel, resort, motel, or motor inn (20%)	1. Go to the beach (including swimming, surfing, diving) (49%) 2. Visit friends and relatives (46%) 3. Eat out/restaurants (46%)
Big tour (8–21 nights)	1. Family group: parents & children (40%) 2. Adult couple (36%) 3. Traveling alone (10%)	1. Older nonworking married person (17%) 2. Parent with youngest child aged 6–14 (17%) 3. Older working married person (14%)	1. Friends' or relatives' property (35%) 2. Rented house, apartment, unit, or flat (23%) 3. Hotel, resort, motel, or motor inn (17%)	1. Go to the beach (including swimming, surfing, diving) (64%) 2. Eat out/restaurants (62%) 3. Go shopping (for pleasure) (50%)
Grand tour (22+ nights)	1. Adult couple (59%) 2. Family group: parents & children (15%) 3. Friends or relatives traveling together without children (15%)	1. Older nonworking married person (53%) 2. Parent with youngest child aged 6–14 (10%) 3. Older nonworking single (9%)	1. Friends' or relatives' property (37%) 2. Caravan park or commercial camping ground (29%) 3. Rented house, apartment, unit, or flat (13%)	1. Just walk or drive around/taking in the sights/general sightseeing (72%) 2. Eat out/restaurants (67%) 3. Go to the beach (including swimming, surfing, diving) (64%)

company car, a rental car, a self-drive van/motor home or camper-van or a four-wheel drive.[18]

The Capricorn region is benefiting directly from the development of the international drive market with local operators reporting that there has been an increase in German tourists exploring the western regions in motor homes and campers. They are being attracted by the ecotourism and adventure tourism opportunities available in Central Queensland.[19] This developing market in conjunction with the $2 million project to establish Mount Morgan as a contributing member of the Heritage Trails Network will provide Pindari with excellent opportunities to capitalize on this trade.

The characteristics of the international drive market are similar to those of the domestic drive market. "Forty-two percent of the international drive visitors to Queensland were travelling as part of an adult couple. Unaccompanied travelers accounted for a further 34 percent of the international drive market in Queensland."[20] Demographically, the international drive market for the Capricorn region is predominately visitors who are between 20 and 29 years old (47%), and the majority (81%) are on holiday.[21]

ACCESSIBILITY, ACTIONABILITY, AND SUBSTANTIALITY OF THE DRIVE MARKET

This market will best be served by Pindari's storefront and major point of sales for products will remain through both the shop itself and through the tourist information center. The heritage experience offered by Central Queensland in conjunction with the Heritage Trails Network scheme will provide Pindari with sufficient through traffic.

The other locations for sales of Pindari products will include other tourist information centers throughout the region and a selection of the region's gift item retailers. (This strategy uses a combination of the indigenous-owned or -operated "gallery" facility and other nonindigenous-operated retail outlets, providing Pindari with the best opportunities for exposure to the drive market within the current production capabilities.) Further locations will be negotiated over time with the continued expansion of the operation.

Benefits for the Consumers

The drive market is particularly important for Pindari as a higher proportion of the revenue from sales is retained by the company or artists. There are a range of benefits (for both consumers and the artists) in providing an authentic experience for consumers of indigenous artifacts, which include the following:[22]

- Tourists seeking some form of cultural experience appreciate the opportunity to see and buy indigenous arts and crafts, and they are estimated to be responsible for over half of all indigenous art sales.
- Tourists place value on being able to discuss artwork with the artist and being able to see artists at work. Opportunities for this type of contact will not only encourage sales but also provide for education of tourists about indigenous art appreciation, helping to cultivate the market for the longer term.
- There is opportunity for innovative product development in the souvenir market.

3.3.3 The Duty-Free Market

The second market segment that Pindari is targeting is the duty-free market, which includes sales to international visitors through duty-free stores and retail outlets owned or operated by nonindigenous operators (initially within Sydney's Darling Harbor and Brisbane's Queen Street Mall stores as test markets). While we do not at this time have detailed information of duty-free store patronage directly (we plan to carry this research out through our own sales), we can make some assumptions concerning the characteristics of the target market by detailing the international tourist market for Australia.

Target Market Overview

In 2001, Australia's inbound travel market accounted for 52.7% of sales for the tourism industry, equivalent to $14.1 billion.[23] In 2002, the Australian Bureau of Statistics (ABS) recorded approximately 4.8 million international visitors to Australia, which were made up of the market segments shown in Figure 3.[24]

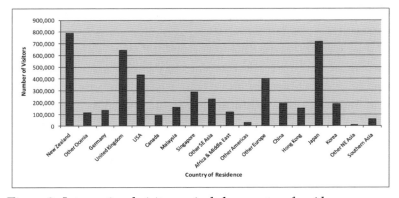

Figure 3. International visitor arrivals by country of residence.

3.3.4 Demographic and Psychographic Characteristics of the Duty-Free Target Market

Of those international visitors to Australia, the total number of visitors experiencing indigenous art and craft and cultural displays was 411,500 (approximately 8.5%). Of the international visitor groupings as identified in Figure 3, the percentage of visitors from each country who experienced indigenous art and craft and cultural displays is shown in Table 6.[25]

This indicates that the Western European markets (Other Europe, Germany, and the United Kingdom) were the largest markets participating in indigenous cultural products and experiences. Visitors from Germany, Other Europe, China, and the United Kingdom were most influenced by indigenous culture in their decision to visit Australia, and of the Asian nations, visitors from Japan and Taiwan had the

Table 6. Percentage of Visitors From Each Country Who Experienced Indigenous Art, Craft, and Cultural Displays[26]

Country	Percentage
USA	16
Canada	20
United Kingdom	18
Germany	32
Other Europe	20
All other countries	The respective percentage for each country was less than 10%.

highest percentages of participation in indigenous products and experiences.[27]

Major market overviews are provided in the following paragraphs and are discussed in relation to the buyer-readiness states model as demonstrated in Figure 4.[28]

Briefly, the buyer-readiness states model provides insight into the phases consumers normally progress through in their decision-making process. At each stage companies should aim to inform, remind, reinforce, or persuade consumers to influence the purchase decision. At the awareness stage, we need to assess whether consumers have any prior understanding or awareness of the product. At the second stage, the target audience may be aware of the product but know little else—companies need to communicate overall objectives or benefits of the product. At the third stage, the company tries to engender a liking for the product in the consumer due to the idea that even if consumers recognize and have knowledge of the product, they may not have a feeling about it. In the fourth stage, consumers may like the products but may not have particular preference for these products over competitor's products (either direct competitors or substitute products). The next stage in the buying process is to develop a conviction that purchasing this particular brand or company's product over others is "the right thing to do."[29] Finally, even if target members have conviction that the product is the correct choice, they may not actually purchase, so companies may need to offer incentives to purchase.

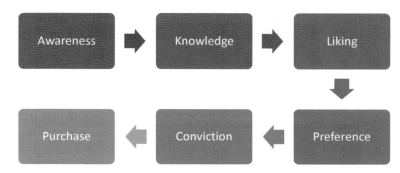

Figure 4. Buyer-readiness states model.

GERMANY AND THE UNITED KINGDOM

Generally, German visitors rate cultural experiences as an important part of the travel experience. Brand audit research demonstrates that German visitors express awareness, knowledge, interest, and curiosity in indigenous culture. German visitors also demonstrate the highest percentage of participation in cultural experiences, as nearly one third of German tourists who visit Australia participate in cultural opportunities.[30] Therefore, the German tourist population demonstrates solid conviction, preference, and purchase behavior.

Visitors from the United Kingdom have a high awareness, knowledge of, and liking for indigenous products and around one-fifth of UK visitors to Australia demonstrate conviction, preference, and purchase behavior for indigenous art or craft and cultural products or experiences. Both German and UK tourists share the preference for authentic cultural experiences.[31] Hence these are both solid target market segments for Pindari.

OTHER EUROPEAN COUNTRIES

Again, up to one-fifth of visitors from other European countries demonstrate a relatively high participation in indigenous experiences. The Other European countries group includes approximately 30 European countries, excluding Germany and the United Kingdom. Other European visitors also demonstrate a high interest and generally a level of awareness of indigenous products. However, producers of indigenous products could improve education in these markets, as knowledge of and liking for these products is low.[32]

CANADA AND THE UNITED STATES

Canadian visitors demonstrate similar readiness and purchase behaviors as the Other European visitors. U.S. visitors to Australia demonstrate a high level of interest in, and awareness of, indigenous products or experiences. However, as with Other European and Canadian visitors, U.S. visitors' knowledge, liking, and conviction levels could be improved.[33]

NEW ZEALAND, HONG KONG, TAIWAN, SINGAPORE, MALAYSIA, JAPAN, AND CHINA

Indigenous art or craft and cultural experience participation for each of these markets is low, although all the countries do demonstrate a basic awareness and some level of knowledge of indigenous products. Educational communications for these markets would help to address these issues, although growth in sales from these segments would be slow. New Zealand visitors do not express great interest in indigenous products or activities (possibly due to their home country's large indigenous population and tourism industry.)[34]

TYPES OF PRODUCTS AND BENEFITS FOR THE CONSUMER: WHY WOULD CONSUMERS PURCHASE?

The international market consists of two major segments, including the export market and "hidden exports" (sales in Australia to overseas visitors).[35] In both of these cases, the market is classified into the following consumer product segments (classifications are supplied by Adrian Newstead, who is a leading art consultant in the field):

- *Fine art.* These include works above a nominal value by a specified list of known artists, which includes paintings (on various mediums), sculpture, public artworks, and so on.
- *Handmade crafts.* These include didgeridoos, weaving, basketry, small sculpture and carvings, ceremonial regalia, and so on. (Didgeridoo sales have increased dramatically in the last decade and are now considered a cornerstone of the industry.)
- *Collaborative products.* These include T-shirts, fabrics and clothing, other wooden "blanks" that are imported and painted with indigenous designs (including wooden bracelets and other jewelry).
- *Associated products.* These include value-adding products, such as books, CDs, cassettes, videos, which provide insight for the consumer into cultural stories and meanings. These products add documentation and authentication to the works.
- *Licensed products.* These are items "where indigenous people are paid anything from a substantial license fee to a miniscule, exploitative one and the product is promoted as indigenous."[36]

As demonstrated previously, the major indigenous product markets are particularly interested in authenticity of experience. While Pindari cannot at this stage cover all the product lines as suggested, we can provide target market satisfaction with authentic, indigenous handmade crafts and perhaps move into collaborative products in some areas. Further, in each of these product lines, it is vitally important to stress packaging and presentation as well as authenticity. Packaging should include presentation stands for the didgeridoos, boxing for boomerangs, and other items. Perhaps a carry bag could be manufactured for didgeridoos, due to the need to carry them on airplanes or store in luggage compartments. Packaging must demonstrate the Pindari logo and information about the products and about their cultural heritage and authenticity identification.

ACCESSIBILITY, ACTIONABILITY, AND SUBSTANTIALITY OF THE DUTY-FREE MARKET

The duty-free market is more difficult for Pindari to access, as we will be competing with other national or domestic suppliers of authentic product as well as imported supplies of unauthentic, nonindigenous product. While the duty-free market will be a profitable market to enter (given the point made previously that over half of the sales of indigenous products are made to onshore, international visitors), the competition will be difficult to challenge. Pindari branding will be very important. Pindari will need to develop an image and personality to uniquely identify it as distinct from other indigenous corporations' products or experiences. For the international market, tourists feel the experience of Australian indigenous culture is very important and often a drawing component in the decision to travel to Australia.

3.4 Internal Analysis

Pindari is a small, nonprofit business operating in Central Queensland. As such, Pindari has very limited human and capital resources that will make expansion of productivity difficult in the short term.

3.4.1 OPERATING PROCEDURES

The CEO and the art director oversee the operation of the factory with staffing as previously indicated in this appendix. While the enterprise has functioned well to date with the limited staff and production capacity available, if Pindari is to be successful in the duty-free market and expand production, it will need to establish a pattern of training and a work routine early to ensure a continuity of product and supply. To succeed in the international markets, Pindari will need to supply a reliable quality of workmanship.

3.4.2 PERSONNEL

Personnel is potentially a weakness for Pindari. However, currently a program is running in Central Queensland to teach young indigenous artists the techniques needed to continue the cultural heritage—which is the mission of Pindari—and staff may be drawn from these resources. The artist coordinating the program is a prominent indigenous artist from the local area. Further, other indigenous artists need to be encouraged to add their specialty products to the core lines, which will enable Pindari to compete with larger competitors that draw from a number of the communities in their respective areas.

PERSONNEL EXPERIENCE AND STAFF TRAINING

- Pindari has an advantage in that a number of the board of directors, the CEO, and the art director have previous experience in running this type of enterprise.
- With the opportunities with government that are available, staff training funding is attainable.
- The art director has artistic experience and skills, and other indigenous artists of note are willing to participate to share knowledge.
- One weakness, however, is Pindari's past experience with the duty-free market, and its experience of other wholesale markets is limited. The art director, along with selected board members, should attend the next trade fair in Sydney next February in order to gain a greater insight into the standard, quality, and style of products offered by other corporations currently operating in the duty-free retail market. We need a greater insight into the developments of the retail market for this prestige market area.

The greatest weakness that Pindari will need to overcome is its lack of marketing knowledge and business administration skills. While the CEO has attended a business administration short course, more training is needed in this area. Further, none in the corporation currently possesses a high level of training in the marketing field, and this is specifically a great competitive advantage that other competitors have over Pindari due largely to their length of time in operation.

3.4.3 FINANCIAL RESOURCES

A further weakness that Pindari will need to overcome is that its financial resources for marketing activities are extremely limited. Pindari will need to look to less expensive forms of marketing and advertising and rely more on product placement or location, public relations and publicity, and perhaps develop an Internet site.

3.5 SWOT Analysis

The following SWOT analysis (an analysis of the strengths and weaknesses internal to Pindari's operations and of the opportunities and threats external to the corporation) is based on information distilled from the research conducted thus far into Pindari's current situation (see Table 7). Strategies will be formulated based on this analysis and on previous recommendations throughout the plan.

Up to this point we have provided a very detailed example to demonstrate the depth and breadth of information and analysis that marketing planning requires if the resulting plan is to be effective and successful. However, the remainder of the plan is less detailed because the range of possible objectives, strategies, tactics, and actions, as well as mechanisms for control and evaluation are vast.

3.6 Strategic Decision Analysis

3.6.1 PRODUCT LIFE-CYCLE ANALYSIS

Pindari products are considered to be in the introductory phase of the product life cycle (PLC), due in large part to the slow sales growth to date. However, the industry may be considered to be in the late growth to early maturity stage of the life cycle, where sales are slowing to their peak. Both of these assumptions, however, will change with renewed marketing campaigns at the international level. The introductory stage of the PLC indicates that Pindari should set marketing objectives to capitalize on

Table 7. SWOT Analysis for Pindari Boomerang Factory

Strengths	Weaknesses
• Unique authentic product • Possibilities of niche markets • Linkages with the Queensland Heritage Trails Network • Artistic skills and talent available • Established location with some equipment currently available • Two well-defined target markets that are accessible, actionable, and sustainable • Access to training and funding for training • Community skills and resources available and accessible (including the university and government departments) • An established board of directors and community network with skills to develop product line extensions • Capacity to develop products based on knowledge of competitors strengths and weaknesses	• Few or no internal operational structures • Generally weak internal analysis • Severe lack of funding available for a number of resources • Lack of marketing capabilities and funding resources for marketing activities • Lack of knowledge of the wholesale industry and limited knowledge of the duty-free market • Lack of financial capacity

Opportunities	Threats

• The possibility of integrating Pindari's product lines into established duty-free market operations in Brisbane Queen Street Mall, Brisbane and Sydney international airports, and Sydney Darling Harbor
• Establishing at least one unique product or product feature such as
  • educational materials (such as cassettes of music and instruction for the didgeridoos),
  • materials offered for schools to teach students indigenous culture,
  • photos of the artists, stories or information about them, or both,
  • local stories and stories about the artifacts or paintings,
  • involving other communities and gathering a larger collection of artworks,
  • some means of export (either by the Internet or by overseas representatives),
  • stories about the community and its heritage/history.
• Certificates of authenticity, authenticity labels, or both that are nationally accepted and accredited
• Professional presentation of the website with the capacity for purchase over the Internet using security features and containing photo galleries of the product range
	• Numerous competitors within Queensland and interstate with similar products and well established operating histories
	• Competitors with established niche markets through localized skills/techniques, types of products, product accessories, or by offering other advantages such as performance or demonstrations of culture
	• Competitors with established Internet presences for online gallery viewing and sales of products
	• Some competitors with international and overseas linkages
	• Competitors concentrated in states boarding Queensland and within Queensland, which directly impacts Pindari's major market segment—the drive market

higher pricing, encourage trial, establish selective distribution networks, and develop targeted promotion to create brand awareness and loyalty in the markets.

3.6.2 BCG PRODUCT PORTFOLIO MATRIX ANALYSIS

The Boston Consulting Group (BCG) matrix classifies products according to cash usage and generation using potential growth rate and relative market share (see Figure 5).[37]

For example, stars have great potential to generate cash; however, they are often expensive to maintain in this position. On the other hand, cash cow products have an established market and good cash generation but do not require significant cash to maintain that position. The BCG matrix for Pindari therefore indicates that the enterprise should focus its attention on maintaining or increasing sales of souvenirs and plywood boomerangs to ensure continued cash flow while promoting didgeridoos as higher-priced products but with potentially less return on investment. Hardwood boomerangs and canvases offer potential for good cash generation, but at this stage they will require much greater cash usage to enable the realization of that return.

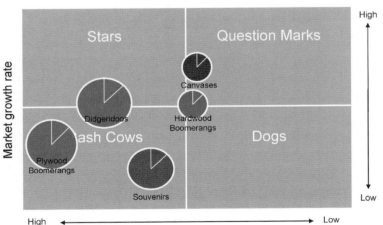

Figure 5. BCG product portfolio matrix for Pindari Boomerang Factory.

3.6.3 ANSOFF ANALYSIS: PRODUCT-MARKET ALTERNATIVES

The Ansoff matrix suggests that businesses have four alternatives in the market: They can increase penetration of existing products into existing markets, develop new products for existing markets, develop new markets for existing products, and potentially diversify by developing new products for new markets.[38] As suggested by the situational analysis previously, Pindari should aim to increase penetration of existing products into existing markets using all current product lines in the existing drive market. Further, Pindari should expect to develop a number of new products through its community artist networks for current markets and it should tackle new markets through the duty-free market through both existing and new products.

3.6.4 BRAND POSITIONING MAP FOR PINDARI PRODUCTS

Based on the competition discussed previously, the brand positioning map for Pindari products shows that Pindari will have difficulty competing on authenticity of products alone and will need to carefully position itself as a cost-effective alternative. This positioning is demonstrated in the brand positioning map shown in Figure 6.

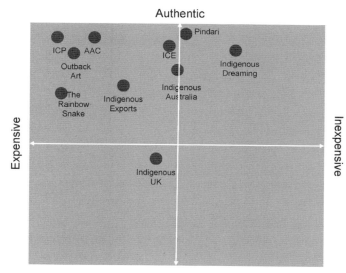

Figure 6. Pindari brand positioning map.

3.7 Marketing Objectives

The marketing objectives are developed based on the corporation's overall direction, mission, and goals as stated in item 2.3. The objectives aim to capitalize on corporate strengths and take advantage of opportunities while minimizing weaknesses and avoiding threats. Thus the marketing objectives are as follows:

Objective 1: Encourage product trial and increase sales of existing products (particularly souvenirs, plywood boomerangs, and didgeridoos) in existing markets—the drive market—by 5% within the next 12 months.

Objective 2: Develop brand awareness of existing products in new markets—duty-free markets—and increase brand recognition to one in three wholesale clients or duty-free retail outlets within 12 months.

Objective 3: Establish sales of existing products in new markets to contribute 2.5% of current gross profit of existing product lines.

Objective 4: Maintain current purchase ratio of 40% among walk-in customers of plywood boomerangs, souvenirs, and didgeridoos.

3.8 Marketing Strategies

To achieve the marketing objectives set out previously, the following strategies have been developed. The strategies are developed under five general areas: (a) product strategies, (b) price strategies, (c) distribution strategies, (d) promotion strategies, and (e) branding strategies as set out in Table 8.

Table 8. Marketing Strategies and Activities

Marketing objective	Marketing strategy	Target market	Notes	Budget
OBJ 1 & 4	*Product strategy.* Develop sample ranges of products for each of the major target markets—therefore, two separate ranges based on the product lines as described at item 2.6.	Duty-free market and drive market	The art director and another board member should attend the annual gift fair trade show in Sydney in February to determine the duty-free target market competitors' product lines and possible avenues for distribution of Pindari product lines. Product lines can be purchased for resale and can be added to Pindari's shop lines to extend the range and provide consumer choice. The art director and a company representative should also visit duty-free stores in Darling Harbor to canvas competitor lines and open discussions for possible distribution points.	To be investigated
OBJ 2 & 3	*Product strategy.* Build up a sample range of packaged and labeled products to use as demonstration items in presentations to stores and agents.	Duty-free market	During the establishment of the sample ranges, Pindari should do careful analysis of the costs for manufacture of each item/line so that detailed cost structures can be entered into the financial information spreadsheet. It is imperative that Pindari understand the financial and time costs of manufacture of individual product items if production on a larger scale is to be feasible. **Note:** Calculations for the profit and loss statement have been performed based on prices set using this method.	To be investigated
OBJ 2 & 3	*Product strategy.* Design and develop packaging for the duty-free market.	Duty-free market	Establish contacts with The Box Company to develop individualized packaging for prestige Pindari product lines.	$2,500

Table 8. Marketing Strategies and Activities (continued)

Marketing objective	Marketing strategy	Target market	Notes	Budget
OBJ 2, 3, & 4	*Product strategy.* Design and develop packaging (such as canvas carry bags with artwork) for didgeridoos. Packaging here can be developed within the community using screen printing techniques for transferring the designs onto canvas/calico materials.	Drive market and duty-free market	If suitable designs can be developed, material can also be used as tablecloths and napkins.	$1,500
OBJ 1, 3, & 4	*Pricing strategy.* Utilize a competitor-based pricing strategy.	Duty-free market and drive market	The competitor-based strategy examines competitor pricing for equivalent or substitute items and sets Pindari's prices for such items at equal or slightly lower values than currently established in the market. This will provide Pindari with a slight competitive advantage and enable easier market entry.	
OBJ 1 & 3	*Distribution strategy.* Develop and maintain minimum product inventory levels of approximately 300 items per line item prior to negotiation with wholesalers to ensure continuity of supply to retailers.	Duty-free market	To achieve the increased output levels required by the marketing objectives for the following 12-month period, Pindari will undertake a recruitment and training program for new casual and full-time staff. Government assistance funding is available through some programs. The aim is to initiate training for five casual staff in the manufacturing of Pindari products with training provided in the use of equipment and painting styles/techniques/designs. These employees will be under the direct supervision of the CEO and current full-time manufacturing staff. The enterprise will need to aim to increase staff by one every 2 months to increase production.	

Table 8. Marketing Strategies and Activities (continued)

Marketing objective	Marketing strategy	Target market	Notes	Budget
OBJ 1 & 4	*Distribution strategy.* Within the next 6 months, establish a minimum of five new contacts for distribution of product within the Central Queensland region to capture the drive-through market on the heritage trails routes.	Drive market	This strategy aims to develop exclusive distribution intensity.	$2,000
OBJ 2 & 3	*Distribution strategy.* Based on the target market analysis, Pindari products should be located at the Brisbane and Sydney international airports and at a selection of duty-free stores in the main mall areas of the cities.	Duty-free market	This is also an exclusive distribution strategy. Each of these locations/stores will need to be negotiated individually to stock Pindari products, and when products become available. These locations should be selected on criteria of visibility, through traffic, store/company atmosphere (being prestige rather than budget), and employee customer service training plans/levels to provide Pindari with the best image through the store.	
OBJ 2 & 4	*Promotion strategy.* Develop a brochure to be placed in tourist information centers throughout Central Queensland. The brochure should be no more than a threefold A4 sheet that presents the story of Pindari and the Central Queensland community, as well as promoting Pindari products.	Drive market	A combined brochure for the day-trip tour is also an option and will require further investigation. Further, develop a story card that provides an insight into Pindari itself as branding.	$1,500

Table 8. Marketing Strategies and Activities (continued)

Marketing objective	Marketing strategy	Target market	Notes	Budget
OBJ 2 & 3	*Branding strategy.* Develop story/history cards to be included with products. Pindari needs to differentiate its product from others developed and sold by different indigenous communities throughout Australia. Develop story cards for each of the products in the range. Other cards can be developed depicting the artists and their stories to be sold with special artworks (canvases, etc.).	Duty-free market and drive market	Branding is particularly important for the international market as international visitors require authenticity and an understanding of the product's origins, the company's origins, and the origins of the people who created those artworks/artifacts. Develop profiles (including personal information/history and photographic identity) of the indigenous artists to be included with products and on storyboards to be posted around Pindari's main operation center. Umbrella branding develops a single brand for all products in the Pindari range.	$500
OBJ 2 & 3	*Branding strategy.* Establish contact with the various indigenous and Torres Strait Islander agencies, including Indigenous Tourism Australia and the Indigenous Tourism Leadership Group, to gain membership to training programs and also to gain brand image and value as an umbrella branding strategy for Pindari products.	Duty-free market	It is particularly important to be regarded as authentic product producers to gain sales in the international tourism market.	To be investigated
Total cost				$8,000

4 *Appendix: Pindari Boomerang Factory Management Structure*

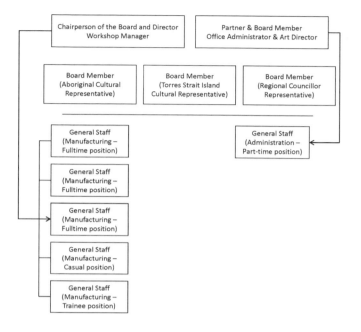

5 *Notes*

1. Aboriginal and Torres Strait Islander Commission (1997).
2. Frankel and Janke (1998), p. 13.
3. Aboriginal and Torres Strait Islander Commission (1997).
4. Aboriginal and Torres Strait Islander Commission (1997).
5. Aboriginal and Torres Strait Islander Commission (1997).
6. Aboriginal and Torres Strait Islander Commission (1997).
7. Hoegh-Guldberg (2002).
8. All organizations noted in this section are fictional organizations. Figures and product lines for the organizations have been developed for the purpose this project.
9. Simpson in Czinkota et al. (2000).
10. Tourism Queensland (2003b).
11. Tourism Queensland (2003b).
12. Tourism Queensland (2003b).
13. Tourism Queensland (2003b).
14. Tourism Queensland (2002).
15. Olsen (2002) in Prideaux and Carson (2003), p. 3.

16. Tourism Queensland (2003a).
17. Tourism Queensland (2003a), p. 5.
18. Tourism Queensland (2003a), p. 7.
19. Tourism Queensland (2003b).
20. Tourism Queensland (2003a), p. 5.
21. Tourism Queensland (2002).
22. Aboriginal and Torres Strait Islander Commission (1997).
23. Euromonitor (2002).
24. Australian Bureau of Statistics (2002).
25. Tourism Queensland (2002).
26. Australian Tourist Commission (2003).
27. Australian Tourist Commission (2003).
28. Adapted from Kotler, Adam, Brown, and Armstrong (2003), p. 416.
29. Kotler et al. (2003).
30. Australian Tourist Commission (2003).
31. Australian Tourist Commission (2003).
32. Australian Tourist Commission (2003).
33. Australian Tourist Commission (2003).
34. Australian Tourist Commission (2003).
35. Newstead in Hoegh-Guldberg (2002).
36. Hoegh-Guldberg (2002), p. 22.
37. McDonald (2002).
38. Ansoff (1957 September/October); McDonald (2002).

Notes

Chapter 1

1. American Marketing Association (2010), p. 3.
2. Ferrell et al. (2002).
3. Ryals and Rogers (2007).
4. McDonald (1989).

Chapter 2

1. Cohen (2005).
2. Reed (1997).
3. Reed (1997).
4. Stevens et al. (1991), p. 60.
5. Reed (1997).
6. Stevens et al. (1991).
7. Hamper and Baugh (1990).
8. Reed (1997).
9. Bell (1987).
10. Hamper and Baugh (1990), p. 28.
11. Reed (1997).
12. Hamper and Baugh (1990).
13. Hiebing and Cooper (1990).
14. Jain (1993).
15. Hamper and Baugh (1990).
16. Hamper and Baugh (1990).
17. Hamper and Baugh (1990).
18. Jain (1993).
19. Stevens et al. (1991).
20. Reed (1997).
21. Bell (1987).
22. Jain (1993).
23. Reed (1997).
24. Reed (1997).
25. Reed (1997).
26. Kotler et al. (2010).
27. Kotler et al. (2010).

28. Kotler and Armstrong (1997); Kotler et al. (2010); McDonald (2002).
29. Kotler (2004).
30. Decker, Wagner, and Scholz (2005).
31. Cooper and Lane (1997).

Chapter 3

1. Kotler, Brown, Burton, Deans, and Armstrong (2010).
2. Kotler et al. (2010).
3. Westwood (1998).
4. Based on Westwood (1998).
5. Burns and Bush (2010); Stevens et al. (1991).
6. Australian Bureau of Statistics (2011).
7. Roy Morgan Research (2011).
8. The Nielsen Company (2011).
9. Arbitron Inc. (2011).
10. Qualtrics Inc. (2011).
11. SurveyMonkey (2011).
12. Stevens et al. (1991).
13. McDonald (2002).
14. McDonald (2002).
15. Kotler and Armstrong (1997).
16. Caudron (1994).
17. Tan and Ahmed (1999).

Chapter 4

1. Hill and O'Sullivan (1996).
2. McDonald (2002).
3. Solomon et al. (2011).
4. Hill and O'Sullivan (1996).
5. Kotler et al. (2010).
6. Kotler et al. (2010).

Chapter 5

1. McDonald (2002).
2. Jain (2000).
3. Jain (2000).
4. McDonald (2002).
5. McDonald (2002).

6. Hatton (2000).
7. Reed (2010).
8. Reed (2010).
9. Reed (2010).
10. Reed (2010).
11. McDonald (2002).
12. Cohen (2006).
13. Reed (2010).
14. Cohen (2006).
15. Cohen (2006).
16. Reed (2010).
17. Reed (2010).
18. Cohen (2006).
19. McDonald (2002).
20. Ansoff (1957 September/October).
21. Reed (2010).
22. Reed (2010).
23. Kotler et al. (2007).
24. Jain (2000).
25. Kotler et al. (2007).
26. Reed (2010).
27. Kotler et al. (2007).
28. Reed (2010).
29. Kotler et al. (2007).
30. McDonald (2002).
31. Hiebing and Cooper (1997).
32. Hiebing and Cooper (1997).
33. Hiebing and Cooper (1997).
34. Hiebing and Cooper (1997).
35. McDonald (2002).

Chapter 6

1. Kotler and Keller (2009).
2. Schoell and Guiltinan (1995).
3. Wilson and Gilligan (2008).
4. Schoell and Guiltinan (1995), p. 287.
5. An interesting article regarding how salespeople can influence product development is written by Joshi. See Joshi (2010), pp. 94–107.
6. For a discussion of the effects of supplier and customer cooperation in achieving product innovation, see Lau et al. (2010).
7. Hasbro (2010).

8. Bradley (1995).
9. A classic book on positioning is written by Ries and Trout (2000).
10. Schreiber (1994).
11. American Marketing Association (2010b).
12. Miller and Layton (2001).
13. Solomon et al. (2009), p. 457.
14. Bradley (1995).
15. Sodipo (1997), p. 123.
16. de Chernatony (2010).
17. Jones (1986).
18. Maklan and Know (1997).
19. Maklan and Know (1997).
20. Doyle (1990); Levitt (1983b); Michell et al. (2001).
21. Keller (2008), p. 51.
22. Schoell and Guiltinan (1995).

Chapter 7

1. Lancioni and Gattorna (1993).
2. Avlonitis and Indounas (2005).
3. Uusitalo and Rökman (2007).
4. Australian Competition and Consumer Commission (2011).
5. Federal Trade Commission (2011).
6. Hiebing and Cooper (1997).
7. McDonald (2002).
8. McDonald (2002).

Chapter 8

1. Reed (2010).
2. Belch and Belch (2007); Kotler et al. (2007); Reed (2010); Solomon et al. (2011).
3. Jain (2000).
4. Jain (2000).
5. Jain (2000).
6. Kotler et al. (2007).
7. Belch and Belch (2007).
8. Belch and Belch (2007).
9. Hiebing and Cooper (1997).
10. Belch and Belch (2007).
11. Jain (2000).
12. McDonald (2002).

Chapter 9

1. Min and Mentzer (2000).
2. Levitt (1983a).
3. Miller and Layton (2001), p. 445.
4. Miller and Layton (2001).
5. Mallen (1996).
6. Bradley (1995).
7. Wilkinson (1996).
8. Hsu, Jap, Liao, and Lui (2010).
9. Coyle, Bardi, and Langley (2003), p. 40.
10. Caputo and Mininno (1996).
11. Miller and Layton (2001).
12. Pienaar and Vogt (2009).

Chapter 10

1. Bonoma (1985).
2. Schoell and Guiltinan (1995), p. 632.
3. Bradley (1995).
4. Waterman et al. (1980).
5. Walker et al. (1996), p. 327.
6. Simberova (2009).
7. Aaker (2005).
8. Ferrell et al. (2002).
9. Martins and Terblanche (2003).
10. Hartline et al. (2000).
11. Ferrell et al. (2002).
12. Wilson and Gilligan (2008), p. 725.
13. Hill et al. (2004), p. 301.
14. Wood (2007), p. 193.
15. Ambler (2000).
16. Ambler (2000).
17. Davis (2007).
18. Farris et al. (2010).

References

Aaker, D. A. (2005). *Strategic market management*. Hoboken, NJ: Wiley.

Aboriginal and Torres Strait Islander Commission. (1997). National Aboriginal and Torres Strait Islander Cultural Industry Strategy. Retrieved April 25, 2003, from http://www.atsic.gov.au/programs/Economic/Industry_Strategies/ Cultural_Industry_Strategy/setting.asp

Ambler, T. (2000). *Marketing and the bottom line*. London: Financial Times Prentice Hall.

American Marketing Association. (2010a). Dictionary. Retrieved November 29, 2010, from http://www.marketingpower.com/_layouts/Dictionary.aspx ?dLetter=M

American Marketing Association. (2010b). Dictionary. Retrieved November 29, 2010, from http://www.marketingpower.com/_layouts/Dictionary.aspx ?dLetter=M

Ansoff, H. I. (1957, September/October). Strategies for diversification. *Harvard Business Review, 35*(5), 113–124.

Arbitron Inc. (2011). Arbitron radio ratings and media research. Retrieved January 28, 2011, from http://www.arbitron.com/home/content.stm

Australian Bureau of Statistics. (2002). Overseas arrivals and departures 3401.0. In Australian Tourist Commission (Ed.), *Visitors by country of residence* (pp. xx–xx). Canberra, Australia: Commonwealth of Australia. Australian Bureau of Statistics. (2011). Australian Bureau of Statistics. Retrieved January 28, 2011, from http://www.abs.gov.au

Australian Competition and Consumer Commission. (2011). Welcome to the ACCC. Retrieved February 2, 2011, from http://www.accc.gov.au/content/ index.phtml/itemId/142

Australian Tourist Commission. (2003). *Segment insights pack—Market research intelligence on Indigenous tourism* (March 2003). Canberra, Australia: Australian Tourist Commission.

Avlonitis, G. J., & Indounas, K. A. (2005). Pricing objectives and pricing methods in the services sector. *Journal of Services Marketing, 19*(1), 47–57.

Belch, G. E., & Belch, M. A. (2007). *Advertising and promotion—an integrated marketing communications perspective* (7th ed.). New York, NY: McGraw-Hill/ Irwin.

Bell, M. L. (1987). *How to prepare a results-driven marketing plan*. New York, NY: Prentice Hall.

Bonoma, T. (1985). *The marketing edge: Making strategies work.* New York, NY: Free Press.

Bradley, F. (1995). *Marketing management: Providing, communicating and delivering value.* Hertfordshire, United Kingdom: Prentice Hall Europe.

Burns, A. C., & Bush, R. F. (2010). *Marketing research* (6th ed.). Upper Saddle River, NJ: Prentice Hall.

Caputo, M., & Mininno, V. (1996). Internal, vertical and horizontal logistics integration in Italian grocery distribution. *International Journal of Physical Distribution & Logistics Management, 26*(9), 64–90.

Caudron, S. (1994). I spy, you spy. *Industry Week*, 35–40.

Cohen, W. A. (2005). *The marketing plan* (4th ed.). Hoboken, NJ: John Wiley and Sons, Inc.

Cohen, W. A. (2006). *The marketing plan* (5th ed.). Hoboken, NJ: John Wiley and Sons, Inc.

Cooper, J., & Lane, P. (1997). *Practical marketing planning.* London, UK: Macmillan Press Ltd.

Coyle, J. J., Bardi, E. J., & Langley, C. J. J. (2003). *The management of business logistics: A supply chain perspective* (7th ed.). Mason, OH: South-Western.

Czinkota, M. R., Dickson, P. R., Dunne, P., Griffin, A., Hoffman, K. D., Hutt, M. D., et al. (2000). *Marketing best practices.* Fort Worth, TX: The Dryden Press.

Davis, J. (2007). *Measuring marketing: 103 key metrics every marketer needs.* Singapore, China: John Wiley and Son.

de Chernatony, L. (2010). *From brand vision to brand evaluation: The strategic process of growing and strengthening brands.* Burlington, MA: Butterworth-Heinemann.

Decker, R., Wagner, R., & Scholz, S. W. (2005). An internet-based approach to environmental scanning in marketing planning. *Marketing Intelligence and Planning, 23*(2), 189–199.

Dibb, S. (1998). Marketing segmentation: Strategies for success. *Marketing Intelligence and Planning, 16*(7), 394–406.

Doyle, P. (1990). Building successful brands: The strategic options. *The Journal of Consumer Marketing, 7*(2), 5–20.

Euromonitor. (2002). Global market information database—Travel and tourism in Australia. Retrieved January 9, 2003, from http://www.euromonitor.com/gmidv1/ShowTopic.asp

Farris, P. W., Bendle, N. T., Pfeifer, P. E., & Reibstein, D. J. (2010). *Marketing metrics: The definitive guide to measuring marketing performance.* Upper Saddle River: NJ: Pearson Education Inc.

Federal Trade Commission. (2011). Protecting America's consumers. Retrieved February 2, 2011, from http://www.ftc.gov

Ferrell, O. C., Hartline, M. D., & Lucas, G. H. (2002). *Marketing Strategy.* Orlando, FL: Harcourt.

Frankel, M., & Janke, T. (1998). Our culture our future—Indigenous cultural and intellectual property rights. Retrieved April 25, 2003, from http://www.icip.lawnet.com.au/ch2.htm

Hamper, R. J., & Baugh, L. S. (1990). *Strategic market planning.* Lincolnwood, IL: NTC Business Books.

Hartline, M. D., Maxham, J. G. I., & McKee, D. O. (April 2000). Corridors of influence in dissemination of customer-oriented strategy to customer-contact service employees. *Journal of Marketing, 64,* 35–50.

Hasbro. (2010). Corporate social responsibility—Product safety. Retrieved August 18, 2010, from http://www.hasbro.com/corporate/corporate-social-responsibility/product-safety.cfm

Hatton, A. (2000). *The definitive guide to marketing planning—the fast track to intelligent marketing planning and implementation for executives.* London: Pearson Education Limited.

Hiebing, R. G., & Cooper, S. W. (1990). *How to write a successful marketing plan: A disciplined and comprehensive approach.* Lincolnwood, IL: NTC Business Books.

Hiebing, R. G., & Cooper, S. W. (1997). *The successful marketing plan: A disciplined and comprehensive approach* (2nd ed.). Chicago, IL: NTC Business Books.

Hill, C. H. L., Jones, G. R., Galvin, P., & Haidar, A. (2004). *Strategic management: An integrated approach.* Milton, NJ: John Wiley and Sons.

Hill, E., & O'Sullivan, T. (1996). *Marketing.* New York, NY: Addison Wesley Longman Ltd.

Hoegh-Guldberg, H. (2002). *The Indigenous art and craft market—A preliminary assessment for the cultural ministers council statistics working group.* Oberon, Australia: Economic Strategies Pty Ltd.

Hsu, J., Jap, W., Liao, C., & Lui, V. (July–August 2010). Build a winning sales and distribution system. *China Business Review,* 16–19.

Jain, S. C. (1993). *Marketing planning and strategy.* Cincinnati, OH: South-Western Publishing Co.

Jain, S. C. (2000). *Market planning and strategy* (6th ed.). Cincinnati, OH: South-Western College Publishing.

Jones, J. P. (1986). *What's in a name? Advertising and the concept of brands.* Lexington, MA: D.C. Heath and Organization.

Joshi, A. W. (January 2010). Salesperson influence on product development: Insights from a study of small manufacturing organizations. *Journal of Marketing, 74,* 94–107.

Keller, K. L. (2008). *Strategic brand management: Building, measuring, and managing brand equity*. Upper Saddle River, NJ: Pearson.

Kotler, P. (2004). A three-part plan for upgrading your marketing department for new challenges. *Strategy and Leadership, 32*(5), 4–9.

Kotler, P., Adam, S., Brown, L., & Armstrong, G. (2003). *Principles of Marketing* (2nd ed.). Melbourne, Australia: Pearson Education Australia Pty Ltd.

Kotler, P., & Armstrong, G. (1997). *Principles of marketing*. Englewood Cliffs, NJ: Prentice Hall International.

Kotler, P., Brown, L., Adam, S., Burton, S., & Armstrong, G. (2007). *Marketing* (7th ed.). Frenchs Forest, Australia: Pearson Education Australia.

Kotler, P., Brown, L., Burton, S., Deans, K., & Armstrong, G. (2010). *Marketing* (8th ed.). Frenchs Forest, Australia: Pearson Australia.

Kotler, P., & Keller, K. L. (2009). *Marketing management*. Upper Saddle River, NJ: Pearson Prentice Hall.

Lancioni, D., & Gattorna, J. (1993). Pricing for profit. *Management Research News, 16*(7), 1–4.

Lau, A. K. W., Tang, E., and Yam, R. C. M. (2010). Effects of supplier and customer integration on product innovation and performance: Empirical evidence in Hong Kong manufacturers. *Journal of Product Innovation Management, 27*, 761–777.

Levitt, T. (1983a). The globalization of markets. *Harvard Business Review, 61*(3), 92–102.

Levitt, T. (1983b). *The marketing imagination*. London, United Kingdom: Collier Macmillan.

Maklan, S., & Know, S. (1997). Reinventing the brand: Bridging the gap between customer and brand value. *Journal of Product and Brand Management, 6*(2), 119–129.

Mallen, B. (1996). Selecting channels of distribution: A multi-stage process. *International Journal of Physical Distribution & Logistics Management, 26*(5), 5–21.

Martins, E., & Terblanche, F. (2003). Building organisational culture that stimulates creativity and innovation. *European Journal of Innovation Management, 6*(1), 64–74.

McDonald, M. (2002). *Marketing plans—how to prepare them, how to use them* (5th ed.). Oxford, United Kingdom: Butterworth Heinemann.

McDonald, M. H. B. (1989). Ten barriers to marketing planning. *Journal of Marketing Management, 5*(1), 1–18.

Michell, P., King, J., & Reast, J. (2001). Brand values related to industrial products. *Industrial Marketing Management, 30*, 415–425.

Miller, K., & Layton, R. A. (2001). *Fundamentals of marketing* (4th ed.). Sydney, Australia: McGraw Hill.

Min, S., & Mentzer, J. F. (2000). The role of marketing in supply chain management. *International Journal of Physical Distribution & Logistics Management, 30*(9), 765–787.

Peters, T. J., & Waterman, R. H. J. (1982). *In search of excellence: Lessons from America's best run companies.* New York, NY: Harper & Row.

Pienaar, W. J., & Vogt, J. (2009). *Business logistics management: A supply chain perspective.* Cape Town, South Africa: Oxford University Press.

Prideaux, B., & Carson, D. (2003). A framework for increasing understanding of self-drive tourism markets. *Journal of Vacation Marketing, 9*(4), 307–313.

Qualtrics Inc. (2011). Qualtrics Research Suite. Retrieved January 28, 2011, from http://www.qualtrics.com

Reed, P. (1997). *Marketing planning and strategy* (2nd ed.). Sydney, Australia: Harcourt Brace and Company Australia Pty Ltd.

Reed, P. (2010). *Strategic marketing: Decision making and planning* (3rd ed.). South Melbourne, Australia: Cengage Learning Australia.

Ries, A. and Trout, J. (2000). *Positioning: The battle for your mind.* New York, NY: McGraw Hill.

Roy Morgan Research. (2011). Roy Morgan Research Centre. Retrieved January 28, 2011, from http://www.roymorgan.com/general/Home.cfm

Ryals, L., & Rogers, B. (May–July 2007). Key account planning: Benefits, barriers and best practice. *Journal of Strategic Marketing, 15,* 209–222.

Schoell, W. F., & Guiltinan, J. P. (1995). *Marketing: Contemporary concepts and practices.* Upper Saddle River, NJ: Prentice Hall.

Schreiber, E. (December 5, 1994). Retail trends shorten life of package design. *Marketing News,* 17.

Simberova, I. (2009). Corporate culture—as a barrier of market orientation implementation. *Journal of Economics and Management, 14,* 513–521.

Sodipo, B. (1997). *Piracy and counterfeiting: GATT, TRIPS, and developing countries.* London, United Kingdom: Kluwer Law International.

Solomon, M. R., Hughes, A., Chitty, B., Fripp, G., Marshall, G. W., & Stuart, E. W. (2009). *Marketing* (2nd ed.). Frenchs Forest, Australia: Pearson.

Solomon, M. R., Hughes, A., Chitty, B., Fripp, G., Marshall, G. W., & Stuart, E. W. (2011). *Marketing—real people, real choices* (2nd ed.). Frenchs Forest, Australia: Pearson Education Australia.

Stevens, R. E., Loudon, D. L., & Warren, W. E. (1991). *Marketing planning guide.* New York, NY: The Haworth Press.

SurveyMonkey. (2011). Free online survey software and questionnaire tool. Retrieved January 28, 2011, from http://www.surveymonkey.com

Tan, T. T. W., & Ahmed, Z. U. (1999). Managing marketing intelligence: An Asian marketing research perspective. *Marketing Intelligence and Planning, 17*(6), 298–306.

The Nielsen Company. (2011). Trends and insights. Retrieved January 28, 2011, from http://au.acnielsen.com/site/index.shtml

Tourism Queensland. (2002). *Regional summary—Capricorn.* Brisbane, Australia: Tourism Queensland.

Tourism Queensland. (2003a). *The drive market.* Retrieved April 25, 2003, from http://www.qttc.com.au

Tourism Queensland. (2003b). Tourism Queensland news—a quarterly journal for the Queensland tourism industry. Retrieved April 25, 2003, from http://www.qttc.com.au/tqnews/issue08/index.html

Uusitalo, O., & Rökman, M. (2007). The impacts of competitive entry on pricing on the Finish retail grocery market. *International Journal of Retail and Distribution Management, 35*(2), 120–135.

Walker, O. C. J., Boyd, H. W. J., & Larreche, J. (1996). *Marketing strategy: Planning and implementation.* Chicago, IL: Irwin.

Waterman, R. H., Peters, T. J., & Phillips, J. R. (1980). Structure is not organization. *Business Horizons, 23*(3), 14–26.

Westwood, J. (1998). *The marketing plan: A practitioner's guide* (2nd ed.). Dover, DE: Kogan Page.

Wilkinson, I. F. (1996). Distribution channel management: Power considerations. *International Journal of Physical Distribution & Logistics Management, 26*(5), 31–41.

Wilson, R., & Gilligan, C. (2008). *Strategic marketing management: Planning, implementation and control.* Burlington, MA: Butterworth-Heinemann.

Wood, M. B. (2007). *Marian Burk Wood's essential guide to marketing planning.* Essex, UK: Pearson Education Limited.

Index

The letters f and t after page numbers refer to figures and tables, respectively.

Announcing the Business Expert Press Digital Library

Concise E-books Business Students Need
for Classroom and Research

This book can also be purchased in an e-book collection by your library as

- a one-time purchase,
- that is owned forever,
- allows for simultaneous readers,
- has no restrictions on printing, and
- can be downloaded as PDFs from within the library community.

Our digital library collections are a great solution to beat the rising cost of textbooks. E-books can be loaded into their course management systems or onto student's e-book readers.

The **Business Expert Press** digital libraries are very affordable, with no obligation to buy in future years.

For more information, please visit **www.businessexpert.com/libraries**. To set up a trial in the United States, please contact **Sheri Allen** at *sheri.allen@globalepress.com*; for all other regions, contact **Nicole Lee** at *nicole.lee@igroupnet.com*.

OTHER TITLES IN OUR MARKETING STRATEGY COLLECTION
Series Editor: **Naresh Malhotra**

Developing Winning Brand Strategies by Lars Finskud

Conscious Branding by David Funk and Anne Marie Levis

Marketing Strategy in Play: Questioning to Create Difference by Mark E. Hill

Decision Equity: The Ultimate Metric to Connect Marketing Actions to Profits by Piyush Kumar
and Kunal Gupta